MORE THAN JUST
THE CATCH

MORE THAN JUST
THE CATCH

DAVID
TYREE
with KIMBERLY DANIELS

EXcel
BOOKS
A STRANG COMPANY

Most STRANG COMMUNICATIONS/CHARISMA HOUSE/CHRISTIAN LIFE/ EXCEL BOOKS/FRONTLINE/REALMS/SILOAM products are available at special quantity discounts for bulk purchase for sales promotions, premiums, fund-raising, and educational needs. For details, write Strang Communications/Charisma House/Christian Life/Excel Books/ FrontLine/Realms/Siloam, 600 Rinehart Road, Lake Mary, Florida 32746, or telephone (407) 333-0600.

MORE THAN JUST THE CATCH by David Tyree with Kimberly Daniels
Published by Excel Books
A Strang Company
600 Rinehart Road
Lake Mary, Florida 32746
www.strangdirect.com

Scripture quotations marked THE MESSAGE are from *The Message: The Bible in Contemporary English*, copyright © 1993, 1994, 1995, 1996, 2000, 2001, 2002. Used by permission of NavPress Publishing Group.

Project Manager: Barbara Dycus
Design Director: Bill Johnson
Cover Designer: Justin Evans, Bill Johnson
Front Cover Photo: © Lucy Nicholson/Reuters/Landov
Back Cover Photo: UPI/Landov
Spine Photo: Reggie Anderson
Editorial Assistance: Len and Carolyn Goss, GoodEditors.com

Library of Congress Cataloging-in-Publication Data:

Tyree, David, 1980-
   More than just the catch / David Tyree.
       p. cm.
   ISBN 978-1-59979-387-0
   1. Tyree, David, 1980- 2. Football players--United States--Biography.
3. Sports--Religious aspects. I. New York Giants (Football team) II.
Title.
   GV939.T97A3 2008
   796.332092--dc22
   [B]
                        check   2008026257

First edition

08 09 10 11 12 — 987654321
Printed in the United States of America

DEDICATION

I DEDICATE THIS BOOK TO MY MOTHER, Thelma Tyree. Mom, through what you have imparted into my life and the love you have given me, I was able to do this book. God's faithfulness has brought us through so much. I will never forget the lessons you taught me in life. Words will never justify how much I miss and love you. You are my number one girl! In my heart, I know that you are watching everything that is going on from heaven. I will continue to celebrate your life until I meet you one day in glory. You blessed me with life...and now I dedicate the story of my life to you!

I love you with all of my heart.

—David

ACKNOWLEDGMENTS *David Tyree*

To Leilah, my beautiful wife and mother of my children: My love for you would fill another book. You recognized the potential in me before I could see it. Thank you for hanging in there with me, baby.

To my boys, Teyon and Josiah: You will be pillars of strength to your generation and will walk in the fullness of all God has for you. Never forget that you will always be my boys.

To my twin girls, Hannah and Sophia: You are identical in physical features, and I declare that you shall also be alike in wisdom and knowledge. I speak a mantle of boldness and authority over you that will be undergirded with meekness.

To Jesse Tyree, my father: Thank you for giving me life. You have been an unbelievable support. God showed out when He chose you to be my father. What you feel for me cannot top how proud I am to have you as a father.

To Bishop Charles Harris Jr., my father in the Lord, and his wife, Janet: You have been a father to me, teaching me to be a man of God. You saw what many could not see, and you continued to speak into my life until it came to pass. Pastor Janet, thank you for showing the love of Christ to my family.

To Apostles Kimberly Daniels, my spiritual mother, and Ardell Daniels, her husband and my friend: I am so grateful that God brought the two of you into my life. My family and I love you dearly. Thank you for teaching us to stomp on the devil's head and live victoriously in the liberty that Jesus has given us.

To Tara and Ron Williams, my big sister and her husband: You have been rocks in our family and examples to me, Leilah, and the kids. We love and appreciate you!

To Jessica Noel, my sister and best friend: Jessica, you have been with me through thick and thin. I am so thankful that we have grown up to serve God together.

To Aunt Bert: Thank you for being the demon-buster in our family!

Your endurance in the things of God has brought the entire family victory.

To Mike and Mark Clouser, my agents: Thank you for believing in me and supporting me through the good and bad from day one.

To Bugadis, my mother-in-law: Thanks for not judging me in my dark times and for trusting me with your daughter. Your genuineness has given us strength to be who we are and endurance to remain steadfast in what we believe.

To Coach Tom Coughlin and the New York Giants: Thanks for giving me an opportunity to be all that I could be in my hometown. I am proud to be a New York Giant. To my teammates, I pray blessings upon you and your families. With our great team and God's help... we did it!

To Eli Manning: Thank you for writing the foreword for my book. You were a big part of "the catch" and know that God allowed that moment to happen.

To Rich Mahler, my financial adviser: I treasure your counsel and call you a friend. Thanks for being a wonderful godparent to my children.

To Grandma Nana and the Tyree family: Grandma Nana, you will always have a special place in my heart...I love you! Thanks for your support over the years. I am proud to be a Tyree.

To Bethel Church of Praise: I started my walk with God with you, and you have been my family outside of my family. Thanks for your prayers and continual love.

To the Bowers-Branch family: Pop Leroy, your example has shown me how to be the head of my house. Jerry, it is official. I love you more! Burnell and Steven, you are the brothers I never had. Kiara, I miss you very much and decree that you shall not miss your destiny. Shanny-poo, you will forever be my little Shanny-poo.

There is not enough room to acknowledge everyone who has touched our lives in a special way. Thank you for loving the Tyree family and making us special in your life.

ACKNOWLEDGMENTS *Kimberly Daniels*

I would like to thank the staff at Strang Communications for all your support that David and I received in making this project happen. *Whew…*we did it!

Stephen and Joy, Danny and I love you and appreciate the covenant that God has reinforced between us over the years. Thank you for grasping the vision of this book and putting me in the starting blocks to run with it. David and I could not have done this project without your prayers and support.

I would not be able to do this book if my son, Mike, was not in the NFL. Mike, we are so proud of you; God used you. When it did not look like it was going to happen, you kept on pressing. Your attitude and spirit of support for your team during the playoffs, despite your injury, were honorable.

David and Leilah, you have been a blessing to our ministry and family, and a faithful son and daughter. I am proud to hear you call me Ma! You stood in the gap for me when I needed a shoulder to lean on. Thanks for trusting me!

Danny, you and the children have graciously supported me from the beginning to the end of this project. You are my pillars in everything I do. Faith, Elijah, and Elisha, you are the best children a mother could have. I fuss sometimes, but I love you and I am so proud to be your mother. You are great kids!

Spoken Word Ministries, you are the best church in the world! I am proud to be your pastor. I cannot forget the leaders and members who have prayed for and supported me during this project. Alisha, Martha, Sonya Carpenter, Jemal, Tamara, Brother Clark, Lakeshia Johnson, and Scarla…you guys have done a great job holding up my arms and keeping the ministry moving. Your faithfulness freed me up to make it happen.

Renaldo and LaTonya Wynn, thanks for the work that you did behind the scenes in support of this project. You introduced me to the

NFL years ago when I became your pastor. I knew absolutely nothing about football, and you broke me in. Your family will always have a special place in my heart. Renaldo, thanks for supporting Mike when he was trying to get in the league. Your willingness to be there for him meant the world to me.

Mr. Cherry, thank you for helping Mike with his academics to be accepted to Florida State University. I will never forget how you went out of your way to assist my son. God used you to get Mike where he is today.

Mr. and Mrs. Mills, thanks for taking my son into your family and supporting him along the way. God bless you and yours!

To every team (Berlin Thunder of NFL Europe, San Francisco 49ers, New England Patriots, Baltimore Ravens, and New York Giants) that God used to get my son into the NFL, thank you!

Coach Bill Belichick, you brought my son into the league and taught football to him. Thanks!

Coach Tom Coughlin, you took the baton from Coach Belichick and gave Mike a chance when all the odds were against him. Mike thinks the world of you. Thanks for your influence in his life.

Jerry Rice, you were the reason Mike signed his first contract with the San Francisco 49ers. Thanks!

David Patten, words cannot describe how grateful I am for your generosity toward my son when he was working out with New England. You opened your home and allowed him to live with you for as long as he needed to stay at no cost. God bless you one hundred times for the seed you planted in my son's life!

Angelo Wright, you did not know Mike when you allowed him to move into your home to attend Jerry's camp. You went far past your responsibility as an agent, and I thank you from the bottom of my heart.

CONTENTS

FOREWORD

This book is a story of the life of a man who lives what he preaches. I have known David Tyree for the past four years. I have taken note of his efforts as he has been an example as a husband, father, and teammate. He automatically stands up as a spiritual leader on the team. He leads prayer in the locker room and never hesitates to reach out to a player in need. David is a hard worker and always does what he is supposed to do. He is one of the guys on the team who is accountable to make plays. When you come in contact with David, you can easily sense the presence of God in his life. He not only talks the talk, but he also walks the walk. I am so honored to have known him as a fellow Christian and a teammate.

The title of this book, *More Than Just The Catch*, is so fitting. I have been involved in the NFL all of my life. Having a father and a brother in the NFL also has given me exposure and insight into what playing professional football is all about. It is more than the MVP status or the world championship. These things are great, but they mean nothing if we are not imparting values into our families to make them strong.

My brothers and I were fortunate that our father retired from the NFL when we were young. I was four years old at the time. My father only did appearances and speaking engagements, so he was able to spend time with us. During this time, my dad made an effort to impart the right morals into our lives. When I was eight years old, I was privileged to have my dad, "the famous NFL player," be my Little League baseball coach. My dad sharing this experience with me meant the world to me. He was not just involved in our athletic activities but in every part of our lives. As long as I can remember, my dad made sure that we attended church every Sunday as a family. My parents taught us that we had to have the presence of God in our lives. Our family tradition was to eat breakfast and dinner together. Every morning our father gave an inspirational message before we left the house for school. At dinner there was no television or cell phones because it was our family time. No other appointments were more important at this time. All of our attention was required so that we could have that special time that knit us together and made us close.

Our family is not rooted in football but in the love that we have for each other. My father never pressured my brothers and me to play football. He taught us that it was important to enjoy what we did. I actually enjoyed basketball more than football, but I was better at football. I never thought of playing football for a living when I was younger. My goal was to be the best football player that I could be in high school. This opened doors for me to go to college. When I started receiving recruitment letters, I thought that it would be nice to go to the next level of the sport and play in college. I enjoyed playing college football, and I purposed to excel there. As I became an NFL hopeful, the idea of having a job that I loved and did not seem like work did come to my mind. The rest is history, and now here I am.

I realize that many players suffer from the peer pressure of the league. Because I simply love the game, some of the pressures most

NFL players have did not challenge me. I live a simple life, and it just does not take much to satisfy me. I also have the advantage of being the youngest brother in my family. I have big brothers and a father who have strong influence in my life. I believe that the strength of my stability as a young football player is rooted in my family ties. They are strong! The impact that my immediate family members have had on my life is unexplainable.

The person who has had the greatest impact on my life is my oldest brother, Cooper. He was a great football player with aspirations to make the sport his career, but after a string of physical symptoms and sports injuries, he was diagnosed with spinal stenosis, requiring surgery that put him on his back and ended his football career. After his surgery, I watched my big brother learn to walk again. I saw him advance from the wheelchair, to the walker, to a cane. Not once have I ever seen him down or heard him complain. It was so inspiring to see my brother encouraged in spite of the fact that he would never fulfill his dream of playing football. He has always been the biggest support to Peyton and me in our careers. Whether we win or lose, we can expect a call from Cooper after every game. Cooper is seven years older than I am, and I call him my "terrific big brother"!

The NFL has always been a great experience for me, but this year was very special. I think that the doubt and negativity we faced at the beginning of the year made us stronger. The attacks turned into fuel in our tanks to drive us into victory. It seemed like the things that we went through as a team drew us closer together. We became friends at practice and even socialized after work. By Sunday, we showed up ready to work. The negative words of so-called experts did not affect our attitude, personality, or performance. Our team and coaching staff willed to fight past what others thought. We believed in each other and the team as a whole, and it paid off in the end.

Many things attempted to push us down as a team, but somehow we stood strong. Even when things happened, we always bounced back. The great part about this year was that we got hot at the right time. Everything else just fell in place. The victory that we experienced was a result of a team effort.

Players like David Tyree did their part, and everything came together in our favor. David led the team in prayer in the locker room. After we took the field, we got on our knees and prayed the Lord's Prayer. These prayers paid off at the Super Bowl game this year. Though it was a great team effort, the unbelievable catch that David Tyree made will never be forgotten. Personally speaking, I will never forget it. The play was supposed to be a post route. David was not a primary receiver, and the ball was not supposed to go to him at all. Plaxico Burress, Amani Toomer, or Steve Smith should have been on the receiving end of the ball in this play. After the ball was snapped, I tried to step up into the pocket, when I felt someone grab my jersey. To my surprise I did not go down. Then it seemed like another defensive player was grabbing me, and I pulled away again. I scrambled to the right and looked down the field to see David Tyree in the middle of the field.

I threw the ball, and David did the rest. It was an unbelievable effort on his behalf. The will that he had to hold on to that ball in spite of the pressure he was getting from the defender was remarkable. The pressure from the defender caused him to land backward with his back bent. He landed with the ball pinned to his helmet with one hand.

At the time of the play I did not understand its magnitude.

Things were happening so fast that I had to run and call a time-out. When I saw the replay of the catch, in slow motion on the huge screen, I realized how serious this play was.

I cannot describe what I felt after the minutes on the clock had expired. So many emotions came upon me at one time. Should I laugh? Should I cry? Should I scream? I did not know what to do, so I did them all! Winning was more than a personal achievement. I was elated that my team won with all of the odds against them. It was the greatest feeling that I have ever experienced. I imagine that it may compare to having your first child. I am sure that having a child is a greater experience, but I have not had one yet. I do know that winning the Super Bowl was the greatest thing to happen to me up to this point in my life.

The catch that David made was great, but as you read this book, you will see that God has been doing great things in his life for quite some time.

—Eli Manning
Quarterback, New York Giants
MVP, Super Bowl XLII

INTRODUCTION

Now to Him Who, by (in consequence of) the [action of His] power that is at work within us, is able to [carry out His purpose and] do superabundantly, far over and above all that we [dare] ask or think [infinitely beyond our highest prayers, desires, thoughts, hopes, or dreams].

—EPHESIANS 3:20, AMP

R ecently I was browsing around in an athletic shop in New Jersey. I heard a conversation about David Tyree of the New York Giants. I joined the conversation without the people in the discussion even knowing that they were talking about me. A lady was complaining that there were no David Tyree jerseys in the store. The man politely explained that the store could not keep the jerseys in stock. As I walked out of the store, it dawned on me that these people knew my name but did not know my face.

God moved so suddenly and miraculously at Super Bowl XLII that "David Tyree" has become a household name. Before that game on February 3, 2008, I had played football for five years on national television wearing a New York Giants helmet and jersey number 85, but no one seemed curious to know much about me. Because of a couple of plays, now people want to know my story.

I have been blessed with great honors during my NFL career. In my rookie season, I was named the 2003 NFL Special Teams Rookie of the Year; I was also a 2005 Pro Bowl selection as a special teams player. Despite this, I was still not considered to be a "big baller" in the league, but I still would call myself a household name. My job as a special teams player had secured my position on the roster, and I was considered to be an asset to the team. But like all other special teams players, I was in obscurity as an individual player. I have always been thankful for the opportunity to play in the NFL, yet there was still something ahead that I felt I hadn't yet accomplished. I knew God had more ahead. Who could have guessed what it was? February 3 in Glendale, Arizona, changed my life! Things will never be the same. Number 85 jerseys are hanging in athletic shops. My picture appeared on the cover of *Sports Illustrated*. What some are calling "The Catch II" (after the "The Catch," which was the winning touchdown reception from Joe Montana to Dwight Clark in the January 10, 1982, NFC Championship Game between the Dallas Cowboys and the San Francisco 49ers) is being talked about around the world. This career achievement is greater than I could have ever imagined.

I give the credit to God! Not only did He allow me to be on a Super Bowl championship team, but He also intervened and gave me a miracle before the eyes of the world.

Can I or you or anyone else explain what happened? Common sense has taught me that some things simply cannot be explained. Even Bill O'Reilly of FOX News confessed on worldwide television that he believed that a higher power intervened at the Super Bowl this year.

I am excited about this book because I believe people need to know the message behind the miracle. Though miracles cannot be explained, I believe that God has a message in every miracle. The message behind what happened at Super Bowl XLII is that it is about *More Than Just The Catch!*

A CALL FOR COURAGE

The miracle of Super Bowl XLII began long before the day of the game. It started early in the season, during a time of transition when our team was moving from the disappointing 2007 season into a new season of tremendous unity and teamwork that we had never before experienced. We were pressing toward the goal of a championship season as a team, putting aside our own selfish agendas and relating together selflessly for the success of the team.

Yet in spite of that, the members of our team seemed plagued with injuries and freak accidents and overwhelming injuries. By our first game with Dallas, twenty-one players were on injured reserve status. Ten of these players had potential to make the team. Just a few weeks after that first game with Dallas, I was injured and had emergency surgery for a fracture in my wrist. I didn't know why all of this was happening, but I sure knew that God knew why it was happening and that only He would have the answer to what we should do about it.

Apostle Ardell, my spiritual mom's husband, called me as soon as I was hurt. He said, "Son, It's time to gird up and find out why God allowed this to happen and what you're supposed to be doing while you are off the field."

I received another call from a brother who encouraged me. He suggested that I get back on the prayer line with the Commanders of the Morning. (See the chapter called "Physical and Spiritual

Discipline [Part I]" for an explanation of the principles behind this daily prayer practice.)

I was not able to go on the field, so I dedicated my time to 5:00 a.m. prayer. I started on the prayer line with the intercessors every morning. My personal prayer time alone with God is and always has been precious, but I had a situation where I needed prayer reinforcement from others.

During those days, the Lord gave me a dream about the strange occurrences relating to injuries on our team. I saw a dark cloud hovering over the Giants football team. I believe God allowed me to know that the injuries were not natural. I do not believe in bad luck. I believe in curses and blessings. It was no secret that what was happening with so many players was not a blessing.

Whatever is not natural has to be supernatural. When a thing cannot be explained and has a supernatural source, the solution to what is happening is God. I turned my face to God in prayer for an answer.

The first game of the season was against the Dallas Cowboys. For the first time in my career, I watched a New York Giants game from my living room couch. As I witnessed my team lose to the Cowboys, a heavy burden fell upon me. I wanted more than to achieve my personal goals as a player. I had a strong desire to see the favor and blessings of God come upon my team.

I felt encouraged to write a letter to my teammates. I remembered the example of my brother in Christ, Indianapolis Colts Coach Tony Dungy, who gave glory to God at the Super Bowl last year. Though it seemed like an unattainable dream, I dared to believe that our team would be next. The Lord inspired me to write the following letter to each of my teammates and to put the letter in every player's locker:

Sept 10, 2007

To my teammates and peers,

For many of the years I have been with this team, I have had the desire to reach out to my teammates and coaches in such a manner as this. Fear of what others think and would say has choked those efforts, but all of that is over! Last night for the first time in my 5 years I watched a NYG football game on the television, and never have I had so much anxiety and desire to see you all do well. First I must say I am proud of everyone associated with that game last night, and I can't wait to get back out there physically to go to war with you! Truly this isn't about last night in that respect.

There are various ways of leadership, and I know the Lord has called me to be a spiritual leader and example on this football team. For many who know me and others who do not, I consider myself a devout believer or Christian who simply loves the Lord and desires for His will to be done in our lives. This is truly in no way an attack on anyone's lifestyle, faith, or spiritual maturity—only an invitation to those who are willing to fight for the faith as we fight on the field.

In a few short weeks I have watched injuries and press speculation try to dictate the destiny of this NYG football team. As I got the report on my unexpected fracture, the Lord really gave me understanding on some things. Simply, since I have been here we have sustained an innumerable amount of injuries that really challenges our faith and ability to be successful each year. Then last night I heard our good friend (Ha) Tiki Barber say, "It's like someone has a voodoo doll and is breaking down this NYG football team." That truly struck a chord with me.

If you believe in God, then that means you believe in spiritual things. I'm not saying someone literally has a voodoo doll, but there is a spiritual dark cloud over this football team, and it's time to deal with it! The amount of injured reserves and other injuries have been ridiculous, and I just don't believe in bad luck. I believe God truly wants to do great things with this football team, but just like anything else, it takes a level of commitment and, more importantly, faith. Faith does not operate on what your eyes can see, but only on what the Lord is able to do. In order for true victory, we must come together to believe the Lord for the quick recovery of this football team, to remove this dark cloud, and to win a championship.

I charge you all with this! If we can really put our trust in the Lord for something that is dear to our heart as this game is, I believe He will deliver. More importantly, this can be a stepping-stone to other important issues the Lord may want to deal with in our personal lives. Last year's World Champion is the latest example of this. Tony Dungy set the standard. His steadfast faith in Christ despite so many obstacles along the way inspired many to put their faith in something other than themselves. *Now it's our turn!*

This is a wake-up call, but also this is a battle cry for this team to come together, trust God first, and then put our gifts to the test. We are already closer than any team I can remember since I've been here. I believe this to be the last and important piece of the puzzle. We still have to strap up and go to war on that field, and we still have to prepare for success. There is nothing like having the assurance that you did everything in your power to succeed. So let's do it!!

Here are two scriptures that are the heartbeat of what I believe for this football team this year:

"Jesus looked at them, and said to them, 'With men this is impossible, but with God all things are possible'" (Matt. 19:26).

"How could one chase a thousand, and two put ten thousand to flight, unless their Rock had sold them, and the LORD had surrendered them?" (Deut. 32:30). This verse declares with the say-so of the Lord that we can come together and multiply our efforts significantly. One can chase a thousand, two can chase ten thousand— *imagine what 53 can do!*

MONDAY SEPT 17 WILL BE THE FIRST TEAM FELLOWSHIP/BIBLE STUDY AT MY HOUSE @ 7:30 PM. MORE DETAILS WILL FOLLOW.

Especially those who are followers of Christ and have attributed every ounce of goodness to Him, I pray this challenges you where you are in your relationship and stirs up a new level of commitment. God will not settle for second place or less.

1st THINGS 1st

Thank you all who took the few moments to hear my heart.

I'm here for all of you. I'm honored when someone asks me to pray with or for them.

God Bless,

David Tyree

COURAGE OF CHAMPIONS

I wish I could say that we had a big Bible study after I wrote the letter, but I can't. A few guys said that they admired my boldness for writing it. But in my heart I had a feeling that God had a greater plan for the letter than any of us understood at that moment.

What I do know is that even though we suffered from injury in those early days of the season, our team became even stronger and more united in our great desire for victory. We encouraged one another, and we refused to let injury or defeat keep us away from our dream of becoming champions.

There will be many stories told of the behind-the-scenes events that led up to that historic Super Bowl XLII game. This book tells my story. It includes the good, the bad, and the ugly. When you finish this book, you will know that its message is about more than a game. It is about a life changed and the One who changed it. I have a responsibility to God to talk about the changes I went through. I am sharing some very personal things in this book, and it is the least I can do. God allowed me to be a part of what some people have called the greatest play in Super Bowl history to provide a platform so that He would get the glory. I believe that many lives will be touched by the truth between the covers of this book.

If you had called my cell phone right after the Super Bowl, you might have heard this message: "You've reached the voice mail of David Tyree, and I know that you probably saw the catch, but what you did not see is that... God did it! Let's give Him the glory!" That's what I want to do.

My motive for sharing my life story in this book is to encourage others to put their trust in God. I want people to know that Jesus is real. I pray that my testimony will release miracles to every person who reads this book. I especially want to shout out this promise to the young people who think it is boring to serve God: *miracles are never boring!*

I also pray that my story will touch the lives of professional athletes who have been distracted and separated from the reality of what success is. When the cameras' flashing lights dim and go out, I cannot be a hero to the world and not be a hero to my children. Also, success in the eyes of men means nothing to me if I am not successful in the eyes of my wife. There is no great career in the spotlight without a great family life behind the scenes. True happiness extends past the winning touchdown or the greatest catch. Great moments like these mean nothing if there is no peace in your heart.

As you read my story, I pray that you will get the message behind the miracle. Don't try to figure it out. God don't make sense—He makes miracles!

MY CHILDHOOD DAYS

L ivingston, New Jersey, January 3, 1980. Thelma Tyree was thirty-one years old, and she and my father, Jesse, were about to have their third child together. My parents were only three months apart in age, but over the years they seemed to grow a hundred years apart in their relationship. My sisters have told me that there was a lot of tension in the house when my mother was pregnant with me. Tara was eight years old, and Jessica was two.

Tara and Jessica tell stories of my family and my childhood that are hard for me to remember, and sometimes even harder to believe. I used to sit around with them and listen to the stories. Many of the details of my childhood can be told better through the stories my sisters can tell. I will allow them to share their stories with you—just as they have shared with me—in this chapter.

MY BABY YEARS

By the time my mother was pregnant with me, she and my dad were having difficult times in their relationship. My sisters have told me that during the time my mother was pregnant with me, there was so much tension in the air you could cut it with a knife. The arguments between my parents were getting worse and worse. From the beginning, my father was not happy about my mother being pregnant again, this time with me. He just did not feel good about bringing another child into a relationship that had grown sour. In addition to the poor relationship between my parents, my father had a drinking problem, which also seemed to be getting worse.

I was born on January 3, 1980, at St. Barnabas Hospital in New Jersey. My sister Tara Williams remembers the day before and after my birth this way:

> My sister, Jessica, and I were six years apart at the time of David's birth. We were playing in the living room when I noticed my mother coming down the stairs panting in a funny way. I asked my mother, "Ma, what's wrong?"
>
> She responded, "Nothing, baby, everything is all right."
>
> I looked at my aunt Linda sitting on the couch, and she did not look like everything was all right. She looked at me and my sister and said, "I'm taking your mother to the hospital; the baby is coming."
>
> We had no idea if the baby was a girl or a boy. We just knew that a baby would be coming home soon. Lois, my mother's friend, sat with us while my aunt and mother went to the hospital. My father met them there. Though my mother was only gone for a few days, it seemed like forever. Then finally they returned home.
>
> I will always remember the day David arrived at the house for the first time. My aunt Linda, my mother, and my dad drove up in a sky-blue Buick. I was in the den when my mother walked in the door with a bundle in her arms.

The tension was raised to an all-time high when Nana refused to give David to my mother. This created what seemed like a war, and it was so scary. I could hear my mother from the car saying, "Give me my baby!" and hear my grandmother respond, "No, he's staying here with us!" Somehow my grandmother just "knew" that my mother was planning on taking all of us and moving away.

The look on my mother's face when Nana would not give David to her will be forever printed in my mind. After this incident David stayed with my father and Nana for a few months until the divorce was final. This situation really put a dent in our relationship with Nana, and we never really got a chance to bond with her.

When the divorce was settled we were all relieved, but the transition left many loose ends. My sister and I really missed our little brother, and when the divorce was settled we got to have him back at home. We were together, and in our hearts that was all that mattered.

GOD'S PROTECTION EVEN THEN

other often took my sisters and me in the car with her while
ove to pay bills or go shopping. She owned an old, beat-up
car that she bought from an auction. The doors could not
ed from the inside in the backseat.

day she had taken Tara and me with her while she went
g, and we were on our way back home. I was only three
and was sitting alone in the backseat. Tara was in the
with my mother. We were driving down the road on
side of Branch Brook Park in Newark. Tara describes
ened next:

And David was a bundle of joy. He was such a be
tiful, happy baby. David had a head full of hair. He
big curly locks. His skin was soft and brown, an
eyes were closed tight. He did not open his eyes for
David was a quiet baby, and he did not cry much
so excited to have a little brother.

From the moment I saw David I took on a
mother figure in his life because I was so m
than him. Helping my mother with the baby
a joy. I had learned a little about babies with
Jessica, but I had not been old enough wh
born to really help—I was six at the time. B
my baby boy. He was quite different from
his age. Even as a toddler he was a loner ar
tained himself. He would sit in front of
for hours like he was mesmerized. His fa
were *Transformers*, *G. I. Joe*, and *He-Ma*
tized scenes with his figurines and seer
up in his own world. He was not a l
with because he was so easygoing.

By the time I was six months old m
Eighteen months later they were legall
my mother custody of the children,
them, although they loved and miss
for the fighting to finally be over.

But it wasn't truly over. Tara re
broke out at my grandmother's ho
to pick me up. Nana was my fath
tension over my parent's divorc
have the greatest relationship a
happened:

My m
she dr
police
be ope
One
shoppin
years old
front sea
the other
what hap

All of a sudden, I noticed my mother's frightened face as she looked into her rearview mirror. She screamed, "Oh, my God, David!"

As I looked into the backseat there was no David. Through the car's back window I saw David rolling in the street. He had somehow fallen out of the car—the backseat car door was wide open!

My mother was frantic, and I was in shock and could not move. Mother crashed the car into a sign at the gas station. As the car sat halfway in the street, my mother ran out of the car toward David as I waited in the car with the driver's door wide open.

I could see an eighteen-wheeler rolling down the street toward David. Instead of running toward David, my mother made a mad dash in front of the truck. She was determined to stop this huge vehicle from running over her baby. It was amazing how she could think and respond so well at the spur of the moment under such frightening circumstances.

The driver saw my mother signaling him to stop and yielded to her warning. It was such a relief to see that truck stop! My mother's attention then went from the truck to my little brother. She grabbed David and pulled him close to her body. She held him so tight that it looked like she was trying to pull him inside her. She walked back to the car, continuing to hold him close. I could see her body shaking. My mother was not an emotional person, but this incident shook her to the bone.

I asked her, "Mommy, are you all right?"

Without looking in my direction, she waved at me with her hand and said, "Not now, baby, not now!"

She drove the rest of the way home with David glued to her chest. To this day we never understood how the back door of that car came open by itself. It never opened

from the inside again, and my mother did not put David
in the backseat under any circumstance after that time.

At three years of age I knew nothing about a God who loved
and protected His children. I do not even remember this incident. But I know now that even at that young age, God had a
plan for my life that did not involve an end to my life from the
blow of an eighteen-wheeler! God had something more in store
for me.

THOSE EARLY YEARS OF SEPARATION

Even though my parents had divorced, my father lived only six
blocks away from us at my Nana's house. He was a big part of my
life, and it meant so much to me to know that he was just a short
walk away. My parents had come to the end of their marriage relationship, but they both made sure that my sisters and I had both
of our parents present in our lives. My father was an accountant,
and my mother worked for the local phone company. Between
them they made sure all our needs were met.

Every moment I spent with my father was special to me. We
had a very close relationship, and I needed time with my dad
more than anyone else—after all, I was the only boy in a houseful
of women! One of the things I enjoyed the most with my dad was
when he picked us up and took us to Plenty's Ice Cream Shop.

As I grew older, I grew very close to my sister Jessica. We were
only two years apart and had a lot in common. Tara, who was
six years older than Jessica, remembers how well Jessica and I
played together, even sharing a room until I was around five or
six years old. Tara also remembers that as I grew, I became more
and more mischievous. I developed a fascination with fire, and
she tells the story of a near disaster because of this:

David was fascinated with fire. I would catch him playing with matches, and we would always find matches that had been struck in his room. One day David was playing around a big tree in our yard that was full of black ants. He said he wanted to get rid of the ants, so he started a fire in the trunk of the tree. The tree began to burn from the inside, and smoke poured out of it. The neighbors called the fire department. After the fire was put out, the fire marshal sat David down and talked to him about fire safety. When David saw how fast the tree caught on fire, it scared him straight...well, almost straight. David never played with matches again, but he did get into trouble once later for playing with a lighter. He'll tell that story later.

GROWING UP WITH MY BEST FRIEND

My sister Jessica and I became inseparable by the time I began attending school. But even though we were close, I was still a regular little boy who liked to be sloppy, hated doing chores, and loved to argue with my big sisters. Arguing with them came naturally to me. I had only little spats with Jessica, but she and I both had problems with our big sister, Tara. Sometimes she acted like she was our mother! Jessica and I called Tara "the warden" because she seemed so strict and mean. We didn't understand the added responsibility Tara had in our home. Because my mother worked hard at a job until late at night, Tara played the mother role until Mom got home. Jessica and I felt that she went too far at times.

Jessica remembers that although Tara enjoyed taking care of us while Mom worked at first, by the time she became a teenager, she began to regret being stuck with taking care of us so much. She could not go places with her friends without taking us. Eventually she began to take it out on us. She started treating us like we were burdens, and whatever she could do to make us miserable, she did it.

Jessica remembers that one day Tara made me so mad that I called her the "B" word. Tara was shocked, but Jessica says it seemed kind of funny to hear me put "Mother Tara" in her place. Overall, we knew that she loved us. She just had a crazy way of showing it. For the most part, we had a pretty normal childhood.

Jessica tells a story about a time when we were playing with our cousin Nathanial:

> David did get a little drama in his life when he hung out with our cousin Nathanial. Whenever David and Nathanial got together, trouble always stirred. One day they were playing in our backyard. Nathanial was swinging a garden hoe from side to side. David ran into the garden hoe while Nathanial was swinging it. Blood gushed out of David's head, and it was everywhere! As David ran from the back to the front yard, I saw blood oozing between his fingers as he held the gash in his head. I yelled, "Mommy, come quick!" At first David was not crying, but when he saw how I responded, he began to cry because my actions scared him. My mother ran into the yard and saw David standing there. He was a bloody mess.
>
> My mother screamed with a loud voice, "What happened?"
>
> We explained that it was an accident and that Nathanial did not try to do it. David was rushed to the hospital. As bad as the gash in David's head seemed, he only got some stitches in his head before coming home from the

hospital the same night. The next day he was in the back-
yard playing with my cousin Nathanial again. David was
a tough little guy.

Like all boys, I had quite a few accidents when I was young.
Jessica remembers another time when I was hit by a car. Although
the car did not hit me hard, Jessica says that I got up and ran into
the grass and started acting like I was hurt. Even in situations
like that, I could be a jokester at times. After all, I was the baby
and the only male figure in the house, and I learned how to take
advantage of situations to get the attention I thought I should get
at times.

THE WORST EXPERIENCE IN OUR LIVES

The worst experience of those childhood years caused Jessica
and me to bond like never before. A few years after my parents'
divorce, my mother decided that she wanted a new beginning.
She sold the family house, and we moved to Jamaica with some
of her friends. Her so-called friends were a couple that she had
known when she was just a little girl. Jamaica was beautiful, and
everything was fine when we first moved there. But the time in
Jamaica became a living horror for Jessica and me. Jessica tells
this story:

> Soon after arriving in Jamaica, my mother had to return
> to the States to settle some final business before she offi-
> cially made Jamaica our home. As she left, she turned
> around and said to us, "I will be back soon!"
>
> Those words meant so much to us because we were
> in a strange land with strange people. But what could
> possibly go wrong? These people would look after us

because they were my mother's friends. At least this is what we thought!

We started school in Jamaica and were just beginning to adjust to our new situation. Just as things seemed to be going well, all hell broke loose. They picked us up from school, and it seemed like a normal day until we arrived home. To our surprise, our suitcases were in shambles and removed from where we were sleeping. The people whom we were living with were standing in the living room area. They were so angry that they seemed to have smoke coming out of their ears. The man grabbed David by his collar and yelled at him, "You come here and tell me what you did with my money!"

They sat my brother in a chair and began to interrogate him like he was a prisoner of war. The woman then said, "Five hundred German dollars are missing from my bedroom drawer—where did you put them?"

As David trembled from the top of his head to the bottom of his feet he responded, "I don't know anything about any German dollars."

The man grabbed my brother, stripped him naked, and started beating him. The sound of the belt hitting my brother's naked body was horrible. I thought that it would eventually stop, but hours later they were still tormenting my little brother. They swore that they would not stop punishing David until he confessed that he took the money. David did have a history of stealing money from my mother's purse. This couple had heard my mother mention this, so they just knew he was the culprit. David had never taken more than twenty dollars from my mother. As I looked into my brother's eyes, I knew that he was not guilty. I heard him yell over and over, "I did not take the money, and I do not know what you are talking about!"

When beating with the belt did not get the results that they wanted, the man and woman brought out a wooden paddle to beat him with. I thought in my mind, "Something is wrong with these people. They must be crazy." It was as if my brother and I had stepped into some horror flick, but the nightmare was real. I thought to myself, "Oh, my God, please let this be a dream and wake us up!"

Finally they stopped beating David, but things did not get better. They put him in an empty room naked. He was on a concrete floor with only a sheet to cover his body. They did not give him any food, and the only water he got was from the sink in the room. This went on for twenty-four hours.

That same night the man who had been beating the life out of my brother had the nerve to take me to church with him! I thought, "I surely do not want to go to church with this hypocrite!" As we drove to the church I was looking for a way for my brother and me to escape. My eyes filled up with tears because there was no place to run. We were staying in a building on top of a high mountain, and we did not know anyone. We were in a strange country that seemed darker every day.

I took a chance to confide in a woman at church. I panicked and started talking so fast that I could hardly catch my breath. I explained that my brother was being tormented at this man's house. This only made matters worse. I believe that the man convinced her that I was fabricating the story. He was furious with me and vowed that I would get what my brother had gotten, but worse.

My heart felt like it was beating out of my chest as he drove me back to the house. In a furious voice he said to me, "You are just like your brother; you cannot be trusted!" I thought to myself, "He is crazy to think I would let him hurt my brother."

This couple began to look wicked to me as time went by. Their faces seemed to transform into images of demons. Their actions were evidence that they were possessed. I was very young, but I knew that something evil was on the inside of these people.

The next day, the couple took Jessica and me out of school. We began to wonder what they were going to do. Would they kill us? Would our mother ever come back to get us? Jessica became determined to fight back. She did not intend to let them hurt me.

Eventually, Jessica and I were taken to the police station and fingerprinted. To this day we don't understand why. We were so confused. Jessica was eleven years old, and I was only nine. Why were they fingerprinting kids? Jessica says that she remembers thinking that it was just a nightmare and that she would wake up and tell our mother about it. But it was no nightmare. Jessica tells what happened next:

> I never did wake up, and next thing I knew I was on the cement floor in the dark room with David. All I can remember thinking was, "At least we are together." Every time they came in to beat my brother I would fight them off. I would yell, "Leave him alone!" Finally, when they went to work, I got to a phone and called my mother the next morning.
>
> We had been given clothes to put on by this time, but we were not allowed to bathe. I hysterically explained the situation. At first my mother seemed as if she had lost her voice. I think she could not believe her ears. Then

I could hear the panic in her voice as she said, "Don't worry; I'll get you out of there!"

My mother immediately called my grandfather, who was furious. He purchased two plane tickets and called the people who we were holding us captive. I remember the man repeating to his wife the stern warning of my grandfather: "I am sending two plane tickets for my grandchildren. They had better be on that plane; you don't want me to come get them myself!"

These people knew my grandfather, and they knew that he did not play. He meant what he said. They snatched us around, mumbling, as they made sure we were cleaned up and taken to the airport.

David and I stayed silent on the plane ride back to America. We could have kissed the ground when we landed! Our mother's face looked like an angel's, and we could see in her eyes how sorry she was for leaving us with those lunatic people. My mind kept trying to tell me that what happened to us was just a bad dream, but the scars on my brother's body reminded me that it had really happened. After that experience David and I were closer than ever.

My sister, Tara, was in the military at the time. My father had signed for Tara to join the marines when she was seventeen years old. As Jessica and I described our experience to her, she said she could hardly believe someone would do those things to children, and she had seen a lot of terrible things.

Our father continued to visit us at least three or four times a week, and he was only a yell away if we needed him. Tara was gone again, but we still had family to bond with. We especially enjoyed our time with our grandmother, Thelma, our mother's mother. My mom and my grandmother were both named Thelma.

Our family was very small, so we were close knit. There was one unique reason we had such a small extended family—both of our grandmothers on our father's and mother's sides had been adopted. This made it difficult to track down relatives because we only had two legs on our family tree. I remember that as a little boy, I always wanted to know if we had any famous relatives in our family. When my sisters and mother told me no, I'd ask them why. Somehow I thought that every family should have someone famous in it.

I decided that I should be the family member who grew up to do something great for our family name. As you read my story, knowing this will help you to understand why that catch I made at the Super Bowl was more than just a catch to me. It was an answered prayer of a little boy who always knew that he had greatness on the inside. It was my aspiration to do more than just make a name for myself—I loved my family, and as its namesake, its only boy, I wanted to do something great that would make my family great too.

Two

ATHLETICS—MY WAY OUT!

I was experiencing a lot of transition by the time I was in middle school. My oldest sister, Tara, was still in the marines, and Jessica and I were the only ones at home with my mother. The three of us moved from East Orange to Montclair. My mother wanted us to have a better education and wanted me to be able to play sports.

Our schools in East Orange had mostly black students, but Montclair was very diverse. There were black, white, Hispanic, and even some Asian students in our school. In times when racism was prevalent in America, I do not remember any issues that related to prejudice or racism that affected us personally. In Montclair people seemed to be treated like people no matter what color they were.

Though my sister Tara was away, she still had a great influence on my life. She was the first one in our family to become born again. Her walk with God was like a roller-coaster ride because she had struggles with backsliding. Tara seemed to do better in God when she was overseas. When she came home, the peer pressure was too much for her.

Once, Tara came home on leave and caught me smoking weed in the yard. She was walking toward me and it was too late to put the blunt (a marijuana cigarette) out, so I just kept smoking. I was also standing outside with some of "my boys," and I did not want to look weak. I could see Tara focusing in on the blunt in my hand, and by the time she was close enough to confirm what she saw, she went off on me! She was crying and acting crazy. She asked me in a loud and angry tone, "David, what are you doing? You are going to mess up your whole life!"

I had no idea she would respond the way she did. She went off so wild that my high was blown immediately. I could not even think of anything to say. I just looked at her with a blank stare, thinking, "Man, she's tripping, and she done blew my high."

She continued to argue with me as she walked off. Then she turned back, shaking her head at me as she said, "You're really not thinking! You're going to mess up your life."

Tara was still trying to play that mother role in my life. At the time I did not think she was cool at all.

Jessica and I felt like the move to Montclair was positive, but Tara never liked the move. She looked at the move from the outside, taking the position that we had moved a step down when we left a house we owned in East Orange for a rental in Montclair. We did have less space in the new place, but there was something about the move that just felt right. We rented the first floor of a two-story house on Washington Avenue, which was a one-bedroom apartment. Mom had the bedroom, Jessica had the dining room, and I had the living room. It was comfortable enough, but none of us had any privacy.

My senior year of high school we moved. We rented the second floor of a multilevel house on Walnut Street. I slept on the sofa bed. Tara said the new place was nicer, but she still did not compare it favorably to the house that we had owned in East Orange. In her heart she seemed to never let that house go. But when I think about it now, I remember that she grew up there. She had a lot more history there than Jessica or I did.

—◆—

As I mentioned earlier, Tara was the only one in our family who knew anything about the Lord. She spoke positive words into my life many times. She boldly declared my future because she had a vision for me as an athlete. I remember her pronouncing, "You will get a college scholarship for football, and you will be drafted into the NFL!"

Tara put a football in my hands when I was seven years old and not even interested in football yet. She was the first one to make me understand that schools gave out college scholarships for playing sports. I was not thinking about sports on that level yet. I was just young and having fun.

Later, though, I did set a goal to pursue a college scholarship. Being an NFL player was not even a thought that I entertained at that time. I was pretty good with numbers, and I felt like I could really do the "college thing." My family did not have money saved for a college education, so I got the vision that athletics was my way out of my situation and into college. My father was an accountant, and I wanted to make him proud by at least getting a bachelor's degree. With each passing year the vision got clearer and clearer. I started thinking to myself, "Yeah, sports will be my meal ticket to an education."

My first opportunity to get involved in organized sports was in sixth grade, when I played on the 49ers in the Montclair Cobra league. I played OK, but I had a fumbling problem. The next year

I tried out for the JV team. We had great athletes in our area, and sixty boys tried out for it. Only twenty-five positions were available and only the strong survived.

Making the team in a starting position as wide receiver was a big step for me. It was exciting going on road trips with the "130-pound traveling team." The year that I made the team we were undefeated. We even played two varsity teams and beat them. My coach said that our team was the best in the history of the league.

Despite my relatively small size, I also played linebacker. My coach was Coach Aleem. He was not just a coach to the boys in the neighborhood—he got involved in our lives. He was an example to us, and we really looked up to him.

As I look back, I thank God for volunteers in the community like Coach Aleem. They made it possible for boys like me to get involved in positive activities and stay out of trouble. Discipline problems on the team were simply not tolerated. Coach Aleem and the coaching staff in the Cobra League ran a tight ship. Coach Aleem would say to me, "Son, you're the hardest worker out here. It will pay off in the long run." He knew the stats—I was not in the top five to seven players on the team, but I was the hardest worker. I was not a player who leaned on my natural ability. Some of the guys were laid back, but I had what some people call the "it" factor. I felt like I had to work hard to achieve my goals. If I wanted that college scholarship, I had to work hard. I would do whatever it took to become successful.

Here are some comments that Coach Aleem made after the Super Bowl:

> David was an average, good, consistent player. He has always been determined to do whatever he set out to do.

He was a focused and well-mannered kid. Actually, these are the kind of players that end up doing well. The superstars with the bad attitudes usually fall through the cracks somewhere down the line. David had one year of football under his belt the year I coached him. He played in the town league with the sixth-graders. He was an average size seventh-grader, but he was tall and had good hands. I knew that the potential was great for David because he had so much room to grow. David was a fun person and a happy kid. His family was one of the families that always came out to support the team.

I can remember certain incidents that made David stick out as a young boy. We had a tradition of pouring ice and Gatorade on the coaches after we won a game. One of our offensive line coaches ran from the young men because he did not want to get dumped on. David was a crazy kid who loved to have fun. He ran the offensive line coach down and tackled him. This coach was a huge guy. When Dave tackled the coach, it caused him to hurt his knee. The paramedics had to come out to the field and take the coach to the hospital. He ended up getting constructive knee surgery. The rest of the year he had to use crutches, and the coaching staff always joked with him about it.

When David's mother died, I called him right away. I knew I had to connect with him more often because he needed someone who could relate to his pain. I had recently lost my mother and my eleven-year-old son within a few months of each other. Not only did we have deep roots in athletics, but I felt like we could relate to and encourage each other in what we were going through.

David and I always got along fine. I do remember the day I pushed him too hard in practice. I knew that he was a hardworking kid, and I wanted to make him press to his limit. This day I knew that I had pushed him too far. There was a play designed for David to run outside, and he kept running inside. I put it on him that day. I could look in his eyes and see he was extremely frustrated. As mild-mannered as he was, I could see the fire in his eyes that day. Despite the fact that David was about to blow his cool, he still remained respectful. One of the other coaches had to pull him to the side and talk to him. David blew it off and continued to give his all in practice.

I have followed David in sports through high school, college, and then professional football. I knew he had the potential to do something great in football because he had the look in his eye. Over the years I learned to discern the young men who wanted it. That is the best way that I can explain it. David had the look! He had a goal, and something inside of me said that he would not stop until he got it.

No one could have imagined that he would go this far, though. Many of the boys whom we tried to help did not welcome our help. Some of them ended up in jail, and some even had worst fates. David came out of the neighborhood with a success story that young boys will use as a model forever.

Three

TRAVELING DOWN THE WRONG TRACK

PEER PRESSURE

Early 1990s, Montclair, New Jersey. Air Jordan tennis shoes—only two hundred dollars! That's the way I thought—just like a lot of other kids—when I was in middle school. I wanted so much to be accepted by my peers.

As I look back, I realize what a blessing it was that my mother moved us out of East Orange to Montclair, though I would not have admitted it at the time. While there was pressure to be like everyone else, wear what they wore, and do what they did in Montclair, peer pressure in East Orange was stronger and potentially more likely to land me in trouble.

I do not think my story would have come out the same if my mother had kept us in East Orange. The peer pressure there was something to deal with for a young black man. In East Orange the trouble was all around us, and it was not just a matter of "not getting into trouble." I could go around the wrong corner and get jacked for a pair of tennis shoes.

The issue is that when trouble comes at you from all sides, it is hard to stay out of it. It sometimes has a way of finding you. It is "survival of the fittest." That atmosphere is one reason for the high juvenile delinquency rate in the inner cities. Young people have to walk out the doors of their home and beat the statistics every single day. The environment they have to deal with is a curse in our communities, and we cannot pretend that it does not exist.

A stronghold of juvenile delinquency is economic struggle. Add it to peer pressure, and you have some of the ingredients that produce the results we see in our criminal justice system. Most children who will become statistics in our criminal justice system get "inducted" before they leave middle school.

A great deception is that children can be under bad influences or commit high crimes only in the ghettos of America. Crime can be pretty bad in fairly decent neighborhoods like East Orange if certain activities are overlooked or tolerated. I found out that even when I moved to Montclair, I had to prove myself so that I would not get my lunch money taken every day. I had to start a few fights and beat somebody down to let the key bullies in school know that I was not a pushover.

The pressure to get that new pair of Air Jordans is strong on the minds of young people, poor, rich, and in between. A boy from a poorer family might dream of buying a pair of them even though he knows that they cost enough to feed his family for two weeks. During the time I was in middle school, the pressure to wear name brands like Tommy Hilfiger, Nautica, Guess, Polo, Air Force 1, and Timberland was more than could be imagined. Children in families with tight budgets could only dream of those things or do something illegal to get them. I was definitely not the best-dressed student in my class. Every now and then, though, my mother would make a sacrifice to get something special for me to wear. She knew that it would put a smile on my face.

Being stuck in the middle of the economic system can be very hard on a family. This segment of society is often overlooked. They have too much money to be called poor and not enough to be classified as middle class. I would not consider my family middle class, but we did not qualify for food stamps or welfare. We could not get free lunches because my mother made too much money. Without the intervention of God, a family in circumstances like these can really fall through the cracks in life. If an emergency such as an unexpected bill or a sudden increase in a maintenance fee comes into play, a family could fall behind and never catch up.

When I was in middle school, it seemed to me like the people who worked hard got punished for making a little money and could never get assistance. The only people who qualified for any kind of assistance were the ones who did not have a job at all. I saw most of them as professional welfare recipients that got over like fat rats. It can be pretty hard on a single mom paying for lunches for three children every week. She might hand over an average of seventy-five to a hundred dollars a month just for lunch money. That much money can be a lot to a single mother trying to make a living. There is a thin line between being dirt poor and barely making it. I thank God for every day that my mother provided lunches for us in school. She did not give us just anything to eat. We had the best lunches and ate well. We always had two sandwiches, two drinks, and two snacks. Because I knew I had something good to eat waiting for me at lunchtime, it was my favorite time of day in middle school.

So there we were, living in Montclair, but the residue of East Orange was in my soul. I had a bad attitude and a chip on my shoulder about the kids there. Like most of the underprivileged children of East Orange, I saw Montclair kids as spoiled and privileged. I thought, "They do not know anything about life. Everything has been laid out for them on a silver platter. They think they're better than the kids in East Orange because they have life easier!" My mind-set was framed by my roots to judge the Montclair kids as soft. I felt they needed to know what it was like to grow up on the rough side of the track.

After living in Montclair for a while, I realized my perception of Montclair kids was a great delusion. After all, I was a Montclair kid myself now. I realized that all the families there were not well off. There were a lot of hardworking people who just wanted a better life for their children.

In fact, the biggest revelation of all to me was that my mom was one of them. It was a great sacrifice, often day-to-day, for many families to live in Montclair, including ours. People moved their families to Montclair because they knew that the environment they raised their children in mattered.

One day not long after we moved to Montclair, there was a kid in my class who was flirting with my girlfriend. I was new on the block, and he acted like he had something to prove by disrespecting me when I was with my girl. He always said little things to her when we passed by. I made up my mind that if he did it again, I had no choice but to deal with him. It was apparent that this kid was planning on making this a habit and was not going to ease up anytime soon.

I approached him and asked, "What did you say to my girl about me?"

"None of your business," he responded in a nasty tone. Without hesitation I hit him in his face. Good thing he was all talk and had nothing to back it up, because I was not actually the greatest fighter. I proved my point that day, though, and looked good in front of my girl.

THE HARD HEADS

Word got out about me, and I was accepted quickly in Montclair. My role in sports also helped build up my reputation. I eventually got involved with a group we called "the Hard Heads." I was actually low on the totem pole, a background cat. It just looked good to have some partners who were tough guys, and I wanted to be accepted. We shaved the hair from our head because we wanted to look like a popular rap group called Onyx. They were hard-core, underground dirty rappers.

When we played their song "Slam," we would slam dance. This was the black version of dancing that the white kids called *moshing*. This kind of dancing was crazy. We allowed the music to take us into a frenzy. We'd jump all over each other like we were out of our minds. Remembering those days, I realize that it's surprising that none of us were seriously hurt.

As I look back, I also see that the young people who danced like this looked like they were demon possessed. The music that the Hard Heads listened to was so vulgar that we could never play it around our parents. We listened to groups called Naughty by Nature and Wu-Tang Clan. We would get into a car and joyride to gangster rap. It usually pumped us up to do something that we would not normally have the nerves to do.

Being bullies was at the top of our list. We looked up to gangsters and thought it was "fly" to be one. West Coast rap was brainwashing us with the idea of being hard-core gangstas. Tupac and all the other rapping thugs were our idols. We wanted to be like Snoop Dogg and Dr. Dre. Even if we knew that we were not gangsta at heart, we had to portray the image.

Our group alma mater was a song called "Throw Your Guns in the Air." We also played another song over and over that made us feel like pimps and that degraded women, which was fine with us. We got high on that song almost every day.

Being involved in these kinds of things was not a desire of my heart. I was into them because I was seeking acceptance. It seems silly now that I wanted that so bad, but the need was real and meant so much to me at the time. I was happy to be rolling with the tough cats that would let me into their world. The truth of the matter was that it was not my world. The things at the end of the road in this world were not a part of my destiny. I was living a double life.

I did have enough sense to keep my grades up in school. I knew I had a bright future ahead in athletics, but darkness was pulling at my soul. I felt drawn to the presence of thugs, and I got excited about cats who did bad things and got away with them. No one ever took me to meet the ones who got caught.

—◆—

You would think that hanging out with thugs would eventually lead to drinking. This was not the case. I got my first drinking experience at home before I started hanging with the Hard Heads. When I was eight years old, my father would give me a few sips of beer every now and then. It was nothing serious to him. I got the sense that drinking beer was part of being a man. It seemed cute at the time, and it was just how we lived. The reality was that alcoholism was a disease that went way back in my genes, and it was looking for a way to creep into my life.

I got plastered for the first time in my life in the eighth grade. This time it was not just being cute with my dad. It was also not because of peer pressure. I was with a friend whom I would hang out with every now and then. He suggested it, and I was cool with it.

Today I know that being drawn to alcohol was a generational curse from way back on my father's side of the family. The Bible talks about how the sins of the fathers can come upon the children. They go back as far as four generations. Exodus 20:5 records the words of God, when He says, "For I, the LORD your God, am a jealous God, visiting the iniquity of the fathers upon the children to the third and fourth generations of those who hate Me."

As a little boy I drank with my daddy. I even drank with my sister sometimes in the name of having fun. Later in my life when I blacked out for hours from drinking, it was not fun anymore.

ONE MORE CHANCE

One night I was hanging out with my Hard Head buddies. We went joyriding in our friend's father's Jaguar. The problem was that we did not have permission. He left the window open, and we got the keys and took off. There were four of us, and not one of us had a driver's license. We all took turns driving. Even I drove, and I had never been behind the wheel of a car in my life. The oldest boy in the car was in the eighth grade.

It was a miracle that we did not get killed or kill somebody else! We got in major trouble that night—two of the four of us got caught when we jumped out of the car and ran our separate ways. The police got involved. I never snitched on the two who didn't get caught. This incident shook me because I realized that not only could I have been locked up in juvenile hall, but I could have also died in that car.

That fast train was rolling down the wrong track to the beat of the music that I was listening to, and the company I was keeping on a daily basis was changing my demeanor. People began to tell me that I did not even look the same. I was getting more and more mischievous. I was trying to be cool but was losing control. I was trying to impress all my friends, but on the inside I could hear my soul crying, "Help!" I often thought to myself, "This is not me!" I knew that there was a better plan for my life. More than anything, I knew that if I stayed on the course I was on, I could forget college.

With all the conviction that I was going through, I still had not learned my lesson. The last incident of trouble brought attention to me that I did not want. It involved a lady, probably retired from her former job, who was a monitor on my school bus. I thought she was ugly, and I hated her. One day she looked around at me, and for no reason I taunted her.

I asked her in a rough voice, "What are you looking at?" She just turned away from me quickly. I was mean to her, and yet I felt no remorse. I wanted to frighten her and seemed to get a joy out of it. My reward was letting all the other kids on the bus see how foolish I was.

This woman had a coat on with fur around the collar. I took a cigarette lighter and began to jokingly flicker it around the fur collar. I did not really mean to set her coat on fire, but the sparks hit the fur and began to burn. I quickly helped to put the fire out as my heart was beating fast. As we scrambled to put the fire out I was thinking, "Boo-o-o-y, am I go-o-ona get it!"

I did. I ended up in juvenile court and received one year of probation on a misdemeanor assault charge. The only reason that I got off easy was because my mother hired a lawyer—which cost her money she didn't have.

Crimes that relate to fire are really serious and can label a young person for the rest of his life. That fact hit home as I admitted to myself how much financial strain I had caused my mom when she was already having a hard enough time. The judge warned me, "If I see you one more time for anything, you will spend the night with me in juvenile hall!" I decided that day that I wanted to go to college and not to jail. I had to make some changes, find new friends, and get a new mind-set. I shifted gears and decided that I did not really want to be a gangster. I got off of the wrong track and began to seek the right one. I did not know where to go, but I knew where not to go. This was a great start for me to get off the wrong track.

I needed help getting off the wrong track and getting on the right one. I thank God now for the support system that helped me to have another chance. I needed a fresh start. My mother, coaches, and other family members were there for me. If my mother would not have gotten an attorney, I probably would have become another statistic.

There are injustices in the criminal system in regard to race. But more than that, many young black men do not have a support system in place when they get involved in criminal justice issues. They need assistance with attorney fees, and they also need positive male figures in their lives to walk them through. Support for probation and parole requirements is a must. A demand must be put on probation and parole officers to do their jobs properly. We will see better results when a checks-and-balances system on the behalf of the ex-offender is in place. Many offenders are not given a fair chance to change. How do you get a fair chance when you can never get a fresh start? Many young men are labeled as felons for the simplest infractions of the law. Once they become felons, they often don't even have a chance to get even a minimum wage job. I have seen too many young men get sucked down the pipes of the system because they simply were not able to get a fresh start.

Taking a young man before a judge with a court-appointed attorney is like telling him, "Face it. You have no future." The attorney usually plea-bargains for a lesser sentence or tells the accused to take the punishment offered. The sentence almost always means the loss of civil rights and a felony conviction. From what I've seen, many, though not all, court-appointed attorneys are a joke.

I have to be fair, though. There is always an exception to the rule. The caseloads are so backed up that these attorneys do not have time to really represent a young black man who made a mistake and needs another chance. Because of the way things are set up, they are forced to push young men through the system like a butcher processes slabs of meat. It is a vicious cycle that feeds on recidivism. The more lives that get entrapped in it, the more widespread the cycle gets. It is a revolving door and a repetition of lives going nowhere unless enough people step in and take the time to really care.

We need to start with our school-age kids. In 2006, 677,346 juveniles were taken into police custody in America. Of those, 140,758 kids (20.8 percent) were handled in the police department and the children were released to their parents. Another 469,670 (69.3 percent) were referred to juvenile court. Another 55,258 (8.2 percent) went to criminal court, and 8,021 (1.2

percent) juvenile cases got a referral to another police agency. That leaves only 3,639 kids, less than .5 percent, who someone referred to a welfare agency.[1]

Numbers in all these categories are increasing every day. Many of these children have gotten off on the wrong track early in life, just like I did.

I often wonder how many potential Heisman Trophy winners, Super Bowl MVPs, and presidents of the United States, not to mention good future citizens of this country, are included in these numbers. To make it more personal, how many David Tyrees are statistics right now? How many of them just need a second chance?

I realize there are many children who will not submit to the help that could be offered to them. But more real than that, just one life put on the right track could change our world. Because I can relate so well, I know that there are at least a few crying out for another chance.

HIGH SCHOOL DAYS

Montclair High School, 1994. I was a freshman. That was exciting enough. But I was in love! I had a new girlfriend, and I could not get enough of her.

What other people thought about me meant everything at this time in my life. I took a break from the fascination of gangster life and got myself into a new kind of trouble. I really started getting serious about girls. I felt like I was growing up.

No one in my family had a car, and we were used to catching the bus, so I did not have that pressure on me. I was not the most popular guy in school, so peer pressure was still an issue. Being on the football team was usually what gave me my "player card."

I thought that I was on the right track with my first serious girl. I was a virgin and didn't know how to even ask her to have sex, but it happened.

I cut my sports activities down to football only so that I could spend more time with her. I sat at her house as long as I could every night. I usually had to go home around 9:00 p.m. on school nights. I had a pain in my stomach every time I left her. I lived to see her the next time. Yeah, I had that "love jones" (crush), and it was bad.

As I look back on the situation, the emotional pressure in our relationship was too strong for freshmen in high school. We started having problems, and the spats got very bad. She went so far as to pull knives out on me in my own home. I recognized she was missing a few screws, and everyone around us knew it too. My friends saw how I was paralyzed by my relationship with her. They tried to tell me to slow down, but I could not hear them. In my own mind, love was all that mattered.

What I did not realize is that it was blind love. I could not see anything clearly, and everything in my life became blurry except her. It was definitely not a healthy relationship. By the time I realized it, I was in too far to do anything about it. With my mom's work schedule and Tara being away from home, I had more freedom in high school. Unfortunately I was not a good steward of this freedom.

Then one day the thing that I feared most knocked at my door. I found out that my girlfriend was cheating on me. At first I tried to deny it, but she cheated on me several times. I really did not want to deal with it.

As reality kicked in, we finally broke up. Her mother took her out of my school, and I had to endure the breakup cold turkey. This girl had such roots in my soul that I went through withdrawal. I thought I would not make it through. My heart was broken into little pieces, and I went into a depression.

I just wanted to be alone and preferred to stay in a dark room. Darkness set the mood of what I was going through, and light irritated me. I tried to sleep my life away. I wanted to see her so bad, and it seemed like the pain would never leave.

I was living under a dark cloud. And then I woke up one morning and the sun was shining once more. I swore that I would never let a girl into my heart that way again. I had a new take on life, and my heart would never be broken again. My confession was, "If anybody's heart breaks, it will not be mine!" Oh, yeah—I still loved the ladies, but my approach toward them would be from a different angle.

My sophomore year began, and I met another young lady. She was sweet, innocent, and cute. My friends joked with me that she was a geek. I knew that, but I liked her, and I did not want to take any chances on another snazzy chick at the time. I was not ready to jump out into the deep, so I took it very slow with my little "homebody girl."

My new girl hung out with the white girls and was a bookworm. She did hold one strong standard—*she was not having sex!* We remained friends, but she was not giving up the goodies. But I had experienced sex, and I had to have some more. I figured that I would spread my oats and meet some more girls.

A serious relationship was out of the question. Why did I have to commit to a relationship when there were girls who would have sex with me without one? This attitude worked great for me, I thought, and I did not have to worry about ever getting my heart broken again. I decided that I would have a main girl, but a full commitment was out of the question. If she wanted me, she had to take my way or the highway. I put iron bars around my heart and was confident that it would take a serious sister to get past them.

I started playing other sports again in my sophomore year. I was really into basketball, and it was my first year running track. I was one of a few sophomores to play varsity football. In my junior year in high school, our football team won the state championship. By the time I was a senior, I was not only the third fastest 400-meter runner in the state, but I was also well established in the football program. I played wide receiver and defensive end. I was small for the position, but the coaches used me because I was fast and they said I had the heart of a big guy. I weighed in at 160 pounds my sophomore year. By my junior year I was at 170 pounds, and I graduated from high school at 180 pounds. Even as a wide receiver I needed to be a little heavier for a college slot. I had experienced a slight detour with my relationship challenge in high school, but I still had my eyes on the prize...a college scholarship.

As I look back at my high school days, I recognize the sacrifice my mother made when she moved us to Montclair from East Orange. We had less room and paid more rent for it. The move was worth the sacrifice in my case because Montclair was a high-profile area for academic and athletic scholarships. The opportunities were just there. All I had to do was apply myself, and I knew that.

Montclair was a kind of an upper-class neighborhood for us. It was more expensive than East Orange. A few celebrities even lived there. Believe it or not, Michael Strahan, who played for the Giants when I was in high school—and still does—lived in Montclair, and so did several other Giants players.

My mother never talked about finances, but I just knew intuitively that she had struggles at times. She would never let us know about her financial challenges. She did not want those kinds of things on our minds.

The day came when I had not just one scholarship offer but many. I was recruited by forty to fifty colleges and universities and received actual scholarship offers from about thirty-five of them. The first two were Ohio State and Syracuse. I was certain that I would go to college on scholarship, so I boldly told my mother to use the money that she was going to use to pay for my college to purchase a car. My mother just looked at me and said, "Son, what money?"

It was the first time she actually told me how the finances stood. My mother did not have money to save for anything. She was barely making it, barely paying the bills, but thank God, we were making it!

I appreciate my mother and the sacrifices she made bringing up my sisters and me. My father was faithful in paying child support, but it only kept us out of hot water. Only God knows what my mother went through taking care of us as a single mother.

I chose Syracuse University. SU was high on my list not only because it recruited me first, but also because SU was winning Big East championships at the time. I also had tremendous respect for Coach Paul Pasqualoni, who is now the defensive coordinator for the Miami Dolphins.

My gift to my mom was that her only son was destined to be a university graduate on an athletic scholarship. I had worked out hard and maintained my grades, and I was on my way. My mother went with me to the school visit, and I will never forget the glow on her face as we walked around my new campus. I'm not sure whose face was shining brighter that day—mine or hers. It was a great feeling!

Five

AN SU ORANGEMAN

F all semester 1998. I was undecided concerning my major, but I was thrilled about playing football for the Syracuse University Orangemen. It was hard for me to believe that I was a freshman and an Orangeman. College life took me down another track on that fast train. The girls were beautiful, and there was excitement every day and parties almost every night. Being on the football team opened more doors to trouble. I did not have to look for girls. They were running me down.

I would party with my boys until I was inebriated, and then I would pass out. Eventually the drinking led to blackouts. All kinds of stuff hid in the closets of my life. I convinced myself, "I am just having fun living the college life!" It did not matter what I did in my social life; I always maintained my grades for football eligibility. This was not hard for me to do. It was simple; if I did not pass my classes, I could not play football. I made friends quickly in college, and I had some crazy buddies on my football team.

Being so near to all those pretty girls on campus, sometimes it was hard for me to concentrate. Every day, smiling girls from all over the nation walked past me. Girls were a weakness, and having so many of them to choose from chipped away at my motto of never getting serious in a relationship with a girl. Couldn't I have fun and guard my heart at the same time?

The quad was one of my favorite places to pass time. Students walked through it as they were changing classes. It was where people met, and even if you had nothing to do, you could sit down and check out the action.

During the first semester I took notice of a girl I admired from afar. She was the prettiest girl I had ever seen, with the "sleepy eyes" that I love. I knew that there was something about this girl that was special. I could tell that she was not just a one-night-stand type of girl.

I had to calculate my approach toward her. She looked like she would not give me the time of day because she did not seem like the flirtatious type. I never got the nerve to holler at her, so I only watched her in the quad for the semester.

One weekend there was a big party on campus. I was feeling real good, probably because I had been drinking as usual. When I drank, it was like a beast in me came out. I did things that did not come normally to me before I started drinking. It was like I became something else, acting crazy with the guys on the team, chasing girls, dancing, and doing what we did. All of a sudden, there she was. The little nursing major was at the party. I thought, "She cannot resist me tonight. I'm ready to make a move on her."

With the liquor speaking for me, things definitely did not work out the way I had planned. I walked over to her and said, "Hi!"

She looked disgusted, as if she smelled the liquor on my breath, and she glanced at me like she couldn't care less. Then she walked away, saying, "I am not interested!"

"I *know* that she did not just play me the way she did," I

thought, trying to convince myself. The party had ended and everyone was leaving. This could be really embarrassing! I am a star football player, and I have a reputation to uphold.

I tried to play it off before the fellas, but her rejection was killing me on the inside. I thought, "I'm David Tyree, wide receiver for Syracuse University! How is she gonna play me like that?"

—∿∿—

As the semester went by, I continued to admire that beautiful girl in the quad from afar. When she rejected me, I just wanted to pursue her more. Later in the year, I found out that she was in my statistics class. I could not help it. I had to try one more time to take her out. I was not giving up. I knew that if the time was right, I could make a move on her that would stick.

Then the perfect opportunity came. She was at another party. She could not turn me down the second time around! I decided to make my move at the party that night. Of course, I was tipsy—it was the only way to be at a college campus party. As I approached her, she looked as if she was thinking, "Oh, Lord, it's him again. What does he want?"

I walked up to her and said, "Hi, do you mind if I call you?"

To my surprise she looked at me and said, "OK."

I was so surprised that I did not even have a pen to write her number down. I asked her, "Can you just give me your number? I will remember it."

She smiled at me like she was sharing a secret joke with herself. I could almost hear her thinking, "I know he won't remember the number. This guy is drunk!"

She rattled off some number real fast. It did not matter. I was not going to forget the four-digit phone number of the prettiest girl I had ever met.

The next day I could hear the surprise in her voice when she picked up the phone and heard me on the line. You can bet that I remembered that number! I could tell that she was still full of games. I said, "May I speak to Lela?"

She responded, "There is no one here by that name!"

I knew that the voice I was hearing was hers—I could never forget it. I said, "Hold up, wait a minute. Then what is your name?"

"Leilah." From that day forward I would never forget her name!

That's how I remember Leilah and me getting together. She has a different version, and she would not let me do this chapter without letting her tell her part!

LEILAH: THE VALENTINE

David needed to let me tell my part of the story, because somehow our versions are never the same. I will tell the story from here on!

After I gave David my number, he called the next day, and I started talking with him. The thing that really got my attention was what he wrote in a Valentine card a few weeks after I met him. It was just a regular card, but the words he wrote inside it were so deep. I still have the card. Here are the words that won my heart:

> I was thinking about getting you a card that was a little more serious, but I didn't. You know I am a silly cat. I'm pretty excited about your breakup, but I also feel your pain if there is some. Right now I'm in the process of

52

making some decisions. Like, who I want to be with and stay with a while. There are only two girls that I can see myself with on this campus right now. And you are definitely one of them. The only problem I see is that you just came out of a long-term relationship and I don't know if you want to get into another one any time soon. The other girl has been more of a friend to me than anything else, and it will probably stay that way. I pretty much know what I want in life when I see it, and I would pretty much say that after talking for a while longer, you will develop to something special for me. I just wanted you to know where I am coming from and how you should get on my team. Whenever you are ready, I feel as though you're cool people and we can get together and make something happen. For now just give me a call once in a while so that I will know that you might be thinking of what I'm doing. This is actually just an introduction of what I would like things to be like in the future. I want you to tell me what your plans are now that you're single. I would not mind being a part of your plan. All I'm asking is that you give me a call if you feel what I am saying. If you don't feel what I am saying, call me anyway.

Your New Man (Hopefully)...............Dave T

I was surprised that David mentioned that he wanted a long-term relationship. These were not words that were heard often from superstar football players. Neither David nor I pledged a sorority or fraternity, so after his practices and games and my studies, all we had was time. He was asking me to share some of my time with him, but I was not sure if I trusted him or not. I had just come out of a very controlling relationship with my high school boyfriend, and my guard was really up. David and

I were talking, but no real commitment had been made in the relationship yet.

Today, as a Christian, I do not believe in premarital sex. In college, though, I had a twisted way of thinking that went like this: I could not have sex with a guy unless we were "officially" girlfriend and boyfriend. If we were, then it was OK.

One day I was standing in the quad talking to a guy who liked me. David stood back and watched. Later, when I walked over and spoke to David, he gently pushed me away and walked off. I could not believe he was showing a little bit of jealousy!

I called David on the phone and asked him, "What was wrong with you today in the quad?"

David answered with a question of his own. "Why were you all up in that guy's face?"

I responded, "How can you act like this when we have no real commitment to each other?"

David sternly answered, "Whether we have a commitment or not, you should know how I feel about you."

I could not believe what I was hearing. "Mr. Love-'em-and-Leave-'em" was getting sensitive on me! David had so many ladies liking him. It was funny that he could give it out but could not take it. I wondered how many girls had stood by and watched while he flirted around. David and jealousy just did not seem to jive.

David and I had our first official "date" at his apartment. We were watching *Martin* on television, and we got to know each other over a bottle of Alizé, a fruity-tasting cognac. It was my first time drinking, and David kept giving me small amounts. He was pouring such small amounts that I started to ask for more. I really liked this wine. I kept asking him, "Could you pour me a little more?" I was really enjoying myself! The wine I was drinking not only tasted good, but it also made me feel a little light-headed.

Eventually I started to feel funny. It was not a good kind of funny. I looked at David and asked, as politely as a drunk college girl can ask, "Can you get me a plastic bag?"

As soon as he put the garbage bag in my hands, I opened it up, leaned over it, and started throwing up. I do not remember anything else. The next morning I woke up in David's bed after sleeping next to him. I still had my clothes on. As I remembered what had taken place the night before I thought, "Surely this guy will not call me again."

But in my heart I was impressed that he had not taken advantage of me when I was drunk. Not only did David call me again, but he had also won my heart.

———— ⚏ ————

Meanwhile, another guy named Charles had a crush on me. He seemed jealous of the fact that David and I were getting closer. He caught me off guard when he told me that David was seeing another girl. He said that David was at her place every day.

I could not wait for David to show up at my dorm. When he rang the doorbell, I yelled through the intercom, "I'm coming down; there is no need for you to come up." I hurried downstairs to meet him and confronted him in the lobby about what Charles had told me.

David was hot! He said, "Wherever you have gotten your information from, it is wrong!" He made it clear that he did not want anything to do with me if I was going to deal this way. I felt

so bad for jumping on him without hearing his side. I apologized
to him for jumping to conclusions.

David and I grew closer as time went by. One night when we
were hanging out, he started putting pressure on me to have sex
with him.

"No!" I said emphatically. "We have to have a commitment."

David said that I was the one holding up the commitment
in the relationship, not him. He was ready to get serious, I
thought!

On April 3, 1999, David and I officially became boyfriend and
girlfriend...if you know what I mean. I was falling in love with
him. But I had no idea of the rough track ahead.

———∕∿∕———

One week soon after that, David and I were at a party at a house
of one of the football players. David began drinking a lot. My
cousin was with us, visiting from out of town, and I had also
invited my friend Kelly, a brunette white girl, to come along with
us.

The party was off the charts! My cousin had an earring in her
eyebrow that had fallen out. Kelly walked upstairs to the bathroom to help her put it back in. They were upstairs for a while.

My cousin came downstairs with a serious look on her face. She
whispered to me, "Leilah, I think you need to go upstairs because
Kelly and Dave are locked up in the bathroom together."

I dashed up the stairs and started knocking on the bathroom
door. The party was at a standstill because I was making a big
scene. I yelled through the door, "Open the door, Dave!"

His words slurred as he answered, "I'll be out in a minute."

I repeated my demand to him again but with more authority. "Open the door...now!"

David cracked the door open, and I pushed it all the way in. My friend Kelly stood with her back up against the wall. She looked pale and very drunk. I thought to myself, "She is not even worth beating up."

David kept saying, "Leilah, nothing happened!" I ran down the stairs and out of the house with David chasing after me. Of course, he sweet-talked me, and we were together again the next day. As much as I hated to admit it, I was hooked! The real problem was that I had given up the goods. Now that I was sexually active with David, I was not going to let him go.

Six

"BABY MOMMA"

Syracuse University, 2000. Leilah and I dated for one very stormy year. I wasn't ready to settle down and get serious about this relationship, and the college life was just too chaotic and overwhelming. Things got even worse when Leilah became pregnant. Neither of us wanted to believe the news. We were juniors in college, and we had no extra money to take care of a baby.

When we told my family the news, my mother took the news well, but Tara had a fit. She thought Leilah was a gold digger trying to tap into my promising future. She confronted me, yelling, "Now you will have to leave school to take care of a baby! You've messed up your whole life."

Neither Leilah nor I could respond because neither of us knew what was ahead. Leilah describes this difficult time:

> All I knew was that an abortion was not an option. I had life on the inside of me! David and I agreed that we had to live up to our responsibility. We were about to be parents, and we had to walk through whatever came along with it. My prayer was that David and I could get married. The thought went through my head over and over again: "I don't want to be anybody's 'baby momma'!"

Leilah and I went through many ups and downs during the pregnancy. Some days Leilah felt like she was not going to make it. She says that at first she had questions about my ability to fully commit to a relationship. But after only a few months of pregnancy, she had no more doubts—I made no secret about the fact that I was not ready to commit. Her pregnancy only made matters worse.

I drank more and more and began spending more time at the clubs and bars than I did with Leilah. The night she went into labor I was drunk. She had begged me not to go out that night because she was four days past her due date and had started having pre-labor pains. I went out drinking anyway. Leilah describes that night:

> The labor pains started as soon as he left. My best friend lived next door to me, so she came and sat with me throughout the night. David finally stumbled in around 3:00 a.m. He began to tease me as I was having contractions. He even tried to trip me as I walked across the floor. As the contractions began coming every five minutes, David began laughing uncontrollably, out of touch with reality.
>
> Meanwhile, I was very much in the middle of reality! It got even more real as the labor pains came closer. David passed out like he was in a coma, and when it was time for me to go to the hospital, we could not wake him up at first. We almost had to drag him to the hospital with us.
>
> Though David was in the room with me, I felt like I was going through my experience with my first child alone. The stench of liquor was seeping from his pores, and it made me feel sick. Instead of receiving comfort

from his presence, I just became frustrated. My mother came in from New York, and her being in the room with us really helped. David did get sober enough to hold my legs as I pushed in my last moments of labor.

The most beautiful sound I had ever heard was the first cry of my son, who we named Teyon. I gave birth to a beautiful healthy boy. Holding my new baby in my arms gave me relief. All that I had been through during the pregnancy and labor was well worth it. I could not tell what was going on in David's mind, but I was proud to be a mother. I knew that David was proud to have a son, but I was not sure about his willingness to be accountable to the responsibility of being a father.

After Teyon was born, Leilah and I moved in together. Nothing else in our relationship changed other than we were shacking up. It seemed like the solution to our situation at the time, but later it only made things worse. Leilah shares how she felt:

> I was in love with David. He had a hook in my nose and really took advantage of it. I knew that David had strong feelings for our son and me, but I questioned his dedication. I could see David did not know how to really love me. His zeal for being a party animal was also a stronghold that stood as a barrier against any commitment to a family. He wanted me to be his "main woman," but I knew he had too many "chicks on the side." I needed more than he was willing to give.
>
> I was living the nightmare I had always dreaded. I was just David's baby momma! I found condoms in his pockets, phone numbers in his phone, and some nights he did not even come home. I can remember calling David. I'd ask, "Where are you?" He would respond, "I

do not know!" Sometimes he really did not know where he was.

David finally crossed the line. He began complaining that it burned when he urinated. He knew that since I was a nursing major I might be able to answer some questions he had about his symptoms. I asked him if he had been with someone else. He swore that he had not.

I suggested that David go to the doctor just for precautionary measures. I was sure that he would not have a venereal disease. Well, to my surprise, I was wrong. He had contracted chlamydia (an STD that can cause infertility) and had passed it on to me.

This was too much! I was hurt, embarrassed, and furious. Other things happened that I am too embarrassed to even mention now, and combined with the doctor's report, they led to the end of David and me.

A few weeks before I was drafted into the NFL, we broke up. After I was drafted, I moved to New Jersey, and Leilah stayed at Syracuse with our son. Leilah was so hurt about the breakup that her pain seemed unbearable. She says that she felt like I had become her soul mate, and when I left, a part of her went with me. She says:

> I felt so empty. A part of me said, "I can be his baby momma or whatever he wants me to be. I just need him here!" Another part of me screamed louder, "I cannot live like this for the rest of my life. Teyon and I deserve more!" This was the battle going on in my soul. I felt like I was being pulled in two different directions, and I wanted to die. If it was not for Teyon, I know that suicide would have been an option.

I just ignored her pain. I made it a point to pick up my son every other weekend and bring him back to New Jersey. Leilah and I decided to be friends for Teyon's sake. Yet every time I walked through the door, I broke her heart all over again. She knew it was just a short time until I'd leave again. She continues the story this way:

> My love for him could not deny him, and we continued to be sexually active. But it was hard to enjoy being with him when I knew that he would leave my bed and go into the arms of another woman. The fear was even worse than that too, because he would probably be with not just one other woman but many. I had always thought that women who got involved with these star athletes were crazy. I had heard there were many such women. It seemed everyone knew about them, and I thought they were fools, but they were very willing to sleep with the players.
>
> Questions continually ran through my mind. Am I crazy? Have I lost my mind? Am I fooling myself? Where is all of this going?
>
> The sad truth was that in the midst of all of these questions, I did not have one answer. I had one-way conversations going on in my mind that went nowhere.

JUST FRIENDS?

Leilah and I had agreed to be "friends," and so she asked me to be totally honest with her. She wanted to know who I was dating. She asked me all kinds of questions about our relationship from the beginning to the end. She thought it would be healthy for us to be open with each other.

So I began to tell her the truth. I was completely honest with her—so honest that I tore her heart apart again. The truth was too much for her to bear. She found out that I had not been faithful to our relationship for even one day. I had other women waiting for me throughout every minute of our time together. It was so painful for her to hear these things!

I began to tell her about my other girlfriends. She says that at first she was not too concerned about them because she thought of them as one-night-stand situations. But when she found out I had a crush on a girl I used to be in high school with, she knew it was not just a "ship passing in the night." Her fears of losing me began to torment her all over again, to the point that she began to feel physically sick.

By this time Leilah had developed a close relationship with my sister Tara. She told Leilah that the Lord had shown her that Leilah was to be my wife. She joked with Leilah, saying, "David is just acting crazy. The Lord showed me that you are my SIL" (sister-in-law). My entire family had begun to like Leilah a lot, and each of them told her they wanted me to settle down with her and our son. Their dream was Leilah's dream, but there was nothing in our present circumstances that suggested this dream would ever come to pass.

And yet as much as it hurt her, Leilah tolerated my unfaithfulness. Whenever I needed her, she was there for me. She seemed to accept being just a "friend" to me, which is what I called her.

I kept telling her, "Leilah, just wait on me, and one day I will be ready to really commit." But in reality she had little hope that day would ever come.

Seven

A TICKET TO THE NFL

April 2003, Montclair. It seemed like things began to get better for me early in 2003. One day the phone rang. "Mr. Tyree, you are a sixth-round draft pick for the NFL New York Giants," said the voice on the phone.

I don't know who screamed the loudest, my parents or me! I had not had high expectations of making it into the NFL through the draft, so sixth round sounded good to me. To top it off, I was in my hometown area. My boys and I were about to set the town on fire!

I did very well on the football field my rookie year. I led the team with nineteen special teams tackles and was named the special teams player on the *Pro Football Weekly* All-Rookie Team. I played in all sixteen games that season and started in the season's final three games.

All this success was in spite of my alcoholic binges. The blackouts were getting worse. I had very little memory of crazy things I had done the night before.

It is a strange feeling to realize later that a substance has taken away parts of your life like that. Leilah told me of times I got out of bed and urinated in the corner of the bedroom, thinking that I was in the bathroom. I was at a point where I had never been before. I knew I had to sooner or later come to grips with the fact that I was a functioning alcoholic, and I really was not functioning too well. Yeah, things were going great on the field, but my personal life was a mess. I felt empty even in the midst of all the money, parties, and women.

Eventually the hangovers started affecting my reputation as a player. I started missing meetings and getting fined for being late. I was fined so many times that I quickly gained a reputation for poor accountability.

One hangover cost me a lot of money. I was so late for practice that I was almost literally flying down the street in my 1989 Cutlass Supreme. I crashed into a graveyard fence. Unnoticed by anyone, I drove off like nothing had happened.

Before reaching the field I got into another crash. This time it was with another car, and for some reason, the car did not stop. I waited five minutes and then took off. At the end of the season, the head coach, Coach Fassel, finally fined me $10,000. I realize I really should have been fined more, now that I think about it.

Then, though, I decided to make up the loss of so much money by selling drugs. I got with a few of the homies and purchased a pound of marijuana. My own weed-smoking was also at an all-time "high"—in more ways than one. I found a nice "connect" to hook me into Purple Haze, a powerful marijuana strain with a big buzz. I was in the NFL, but I still had the East Orange mentality. This was keeping it real in my eyes.

Playing football so close to home turned into a curse instead of a blessing. What was I thinking? Talk about being slow to get the message—I smoked more dope than I sold. Dealing drugs was not on my list of things that I wanted to do when I grew up. I would have never imagined it, but I blamed what I was doing on the pressures of life that make you do things you swore you would never do. I convinced myself in my mind, "You are not like the rest of the dealers. You just need a big hit, and you will be out of it."

I still was not at the point of understanding that money only enhanced what was already rooted in your heart. My heart's desire was to have all the power, wealth, and women that I could get while I was a professional football player. Many people think that just because players are in the NFL, they are rich. This was far from the truth in my case. After the Giants drafted me, I went from being broke to having just enough money to get me in trouble.

It might be surprising for you to know I prayed the sinner's prayer during this time in my life, but Jesus was not Lord. I made a confession to the Lord with my mouth but allowed the idols of the world to fill my heart, and so there was no room for God.

FROM THE FIELD TO A JAIL CELL

One day I was riding with two of my buddies, and we got pulled over on the highway crossing the bridge in Ft. Lee, New Jersey. We had just finished smoking, and the scent was strong on our clothes and throughout the car. I had just purchased a half pound of bud, and it was stashed under the seat. The officer suspiciously asked, "Do you have anything on you that I ought to know about?"

"No," I answered hesitantly. When the officer asked the same question a second time, I knew we were in trouble.

The officer began to search our vehicle and immediately found the bag of weed. We did not have a few blunts—we had enough marijuana that we could have been charged with the intention to distribute.

As reality settled into my mind that I was going to jail, I wanted to cry out, "Oh, my God!" I thought it was probably too late to call on Him since I was going down for more than simple possession.

I will never forget experiencing the sickest feeling that I have ever felt in my life. I can still remember the disgust and shame that I felt. In my mind I heard a reporter announcing my arrest on ESPN: "Coming up next: Rookie New York Giants player arrested on marijuana possession."

I immediately began to regret playing football so close to home. I was bringing shame on my family, my team, and my community. As I was being fingerprinted, I decided to tell the officers that I was a football player with the New York Giants. This did not do me a bit of good. They looked at me as if I was a good catch for them.

In fact, they began treating me worse than the other guys. "Yeah, big baller, you done got yourself in a bind. You won't be catching footballs for a long time. Son, you won't be catching nothing but time!" They taunted me, made fun of me, and separated me from my friends.

So there I sat in a holding cell, and there was no one in there but me and God. Football was my deepest heart's desire, and I was about to lose it. I had a road-to-Damascus meeting with God there. I cried out to Him, "Lord, I don't know what to do, but I need You. If You could spare my job, I would really appreciate it."

I was hurting in the depths of my soul, but I meant every word that I prayed. I was in a real bind, and I knew it. I was about to be put out of the NFL. I did not know what to say to Leilah. We were not really "together," but she was the mother of my son, and she deserved better.

The pain of fame had begun to take its toll on me. All of a sudden it was not so much of a blessing playing in the NFL in my hometown. It seemed that I was trapped in a glass room and everyone was looking at me. Things were not like they were before. I had become a public figure, and my life was not my own. I was not just a young man in trouble. I was David Tyree, the star special teams guy of the New York Giants. I needed to act like it.

STEPPING UP TO MANHOOD

This became the most difficult time ever in our lives. We were so young and had so many major decisions to make. I had made so many wrong choices. My bad decisions were affecting not only myself but also everyone who loved me.

Leilah was head over heels in love with me. She says that as much as it hurt, she loved me enough to give me an ultimatum. "If he continues down the path he is going, I cannot commit to be there for him," she decided. She never wanted to be just a baby momma. She wanted to be Mrs. David Tyree, and she was not willing to settle for anything less.

But just when she had made up her mind to have a serious talk with me about our relationship, another situation arose. Leilah was one month late for her menstrual cycle. "Maybe it's just stress!" she thought to herself. "There is no way I could be pregnant with a second child from David."

But she quickly found out that she was wrong. A home pregnancy test confirmed her fear. She was already depressed and emotionally messed up because of what we were going through in our relationship. Supposedly we were not "together," but we were still sleeping together whenever I visited Teyon. She describes this time:

> The pressure was beginning to be more than I could bear. The way it was, the relationship was only a license for David to sleep with other girls and get away with it.
>
> I was concerned that I had not heard from David and that he was not returning my text messages. I texted a message to him: "IM with child." (Later I found out that David didn't look at the message until he got out of the jail cell. Then he misunderstood the message—he thought I was texting him about being somewhere with someone's child and that I had left out a word!) I never received a response back. I started to worry, and I called David's sister Jessica to ask her if she had heard from David.
>
> I could not believe my ears when she said to me, "Dave was busted and he is locked up in jail." The words she spoke shook my soul. I had just received the news that I was pregnant, and then I found out that David was in jail. As much as I was trying to avoid "baby momma drama," stuff just kept happening all around me. David had been arrested on a drug charge.

I only spent one night in jail and was released the next day. My career was on the line, and I was even facing possible time in prison. In spite of my problems with the law, Leilah kept insisting on more commitment from me. She was not willing to have our second baby under the circumstances we were facing.

Soon after I posted bail, I was released from jail. Immediately I tried to drown my problems with a bottle of Remy Martin VSOP. I settled down with my cognac and started to mellow out a bit.

Leilah took this opportunity to talk to me heart to heart. "Did you get my text message?" she asked.

"What text message?" I responded.

Without hesitation, she replied, "The message that I sent telling you that I am pregnant with your second child."

Before the news had settled in, she continued by telling me she could not repeat what she had been through when she was pregnant with Teyon. She said, "I need you to make a choice and commit to the relationship or not."

A battle was raging inside me as a result of her news. In my heart I loved Leilah and my son, and I wanted to do the right and honorable thing and make a commitment to her. But I was so used to being with other women that my flesh was fighting against what my heart was saying. I just sat there quietly for a few minutes. Then, softly, I replied, "Everything is going to be all right, honey. I'm about to make some drastic changes." At that moment I meant it with all my heart.

Leilah had heard what her heart longed to hear. She remembers that right then, although she had worries about how long I would be able to remain faithful to my commitment, she was knee-deep into the situation and needed a commitment for both Teyon's and her sakes. She had no choice but to believe that "everything would be all right." In her mind, she desperately wanted to believe me!

Leilah told me that news of my arrest had spread in Syracuse and that the story was highlighted in the local newspaper. She was a nurse in the city, and people who knew of our relationship started asking her if everything was all right. Some of the people who asked questions were honestly concerned about my situation, but others just categorized me as one of those "wild football players."

Rumors quickly spread throughout Montclair, where I had gone to high school, and because of this one incident I went from being a "hometown hero" to a disgrace to the community.

The Miracle Begins

Immediately after the arrest, I went up to Syracuse to visit Leilah and clear my head for what needed to occur next. When I walked into Leilah's bedroom, I saw a Bible laying on her bed. For the first time I began to read the Bible, and it actually made sense. Later that evening we began to discuss our future, and that is when she hit me with the boom bang (ultimatum)! She made it very clear that she would not endure the same hardships we went through with Teyon. At that point I took a deep gulp and made a commitment that we would be together. I didn't plan on making this commitment when I went to Syracuse, but on my way back home God gave me the strength to call every girl I had been involved with to let them know I was getting married.

Concerns about my sincerity began to dissolve, however, because the miracle of change had begun to happen in my life. About a week after the arrest, I hooked up with Leilah's brother to share a twelve pack of Corona. I drank my first beer and went for another, but after a few swallows it no longer tasted the same. God literally took the taste of alcohol out of my mouth. Trust me; I am not the guy who leaves empty beers around, especially Coronas. From that day forward I never desired or struggled with alcohol again.

The following Sunday, March 14, 2004, I walked into Bethel Church of Love and Praise a dejected NFL athlete and walked out a new creation in Christ Jesus. My mother and Aunt Juanita accompanied me to service that morning. I wasn't expecting much more than to get started on a new path. I sat toward the back as praise and worship went forth, and I couldn't take my eyes off of this one particular woman. Her face was illuminated with so much joy as she sang unto her God. At this moment I realized that almost every man in the church would probably trade positions with me, a young NFL athlete with a promising career. For all the accolades I accrued, the women I slept with, and the partying I did, which summed up to nothing, in the end I had no joy! I wanted what that woman had. I felt tears welling up in my eyes, and I tried to sit up tall and be a "man." I could do nothing but surrender as I balled up into a fetal position and wept for twenty minutes. There was such a release, and already I felt a sense of freedom. No longer were these my burdens to bear; Jesus did the work! Later in the service I made a public confession that Jesus is my Lord, and I have never been the same since!

Leilah saw my determination to let God change my life. Although she had not yet given her own life to Christ, she knew that there was a God—she just did not know how to get to Him. She was so consumed with our situation and did not know how to give her life and this situation over to the Lord.

I had a fresh new love in my heart for Leilah and Teyon and our unborn child. God showed me that she was the woman that I was to spend the rest of my life with. I proposed to Leilah in front of my entire family, and we were married a few months later.

We had a small wedding at our church. With a new mortgage, lawyer fees, team fines, and a sixth-round-draft-pick rookie salary, I did not have a lot of money. The money Leilah made as a nurse had been paying the bills for her to live in Syracuse. But

I bought a pretty ring for her, and our godparents paid for a nice dress for her. Our pastor married us for free. We did not even have a honeymoon. We had no money and planned to go home after the service. However, our parents put some money together and took us out to eat. Leilah told me that for the first time ever, she felt sure that our future was secure.

I felt terrible for all the hurt that I had brought to Leilah and our son, and for all I had put them through in our relationship. I was extremely disappointed in myself after the arrest. I really repented and turned my life around in the opposite direction. I swore to Leilah that I never wanted to see a bag of weed again in my life.

God answered my prayers, and somehow the drug charges against me were dropped. I never discussed the details of the situation with Leilah or anyone else. I was just glad that the ordeal was over.

By this time, Coach Tom Coughlin had just taken over as the new head coach for the Giants. I went in to see Coach Coughlin about my arrest charges and told him, "Coach, I've already made some big changes in my life."

Coach Coughlin looked at me sternly and said, "Son, you'd better!"

Not many people believed the change in my life would be that significant. My character was blemished, and it was only my faith in God that made me believe I could change. But God came through for me and delivered me from women, alcohol, drugs, and everything else that can cause the pain of fame in the NFL. We were so glad that this chapter in our life had ended!

But I had no idea that I wasn't out of hot water yet. The devil had a firm grip on me and was not willing to allow me to tiptoe through the tulips quietly into Christianity. In the days ahead, he came against me in a way that I least expected. None of us were ready for the two weeks of hell that I would soon go through after I gave my life to God.

Eight

FROM FREEDOM TO BONDAGE TO FREEDOM

In the days ahead, right after I gave my life to God, the reality of the truth in Galatians 5:1 would become very evident to me and those who were closest to me. That verse says, "Stand fast therefore in the liberty by which Christ has made us free, and do not be entangled again with a yoke of bondage."

I quickly went from one type of bondage to another. I went from the bondage of the world to a kind of "religious fanatic" bondage. I know now that in the eyes of God, it is all bondage. He wants for us to be free indeed!

Because this period robbed me of much of my rational thinking, it is best told through the eyes of Leilah and others who walked with me through it. Leilah was the first to recognize that everything was just not right in my thoughts and actions. She relates the story this way:

> I noticed that David began acting a little strange, but I did not yet know much about Christianity. I thought he was just going through a "Jesus thing" that I did not understand. I knew that something was really wrong, though, when David said to me, "I cannot talk to you a

lot because God has me in training to be His disciple." He constantly called me, crying and apologizing for how he had cheated on me. He seemed to be developing an obsession with apologizing, and I became really concerned. David would only talk to me five minutes a day. He told me, "God has limited the time that I can talk to you so that I can complete my discipleship training."

The situation grew even more serious when my mother called and said, "Leilah, something is wrong with David. He was talking crazy and was really mean to me. This is not David's personality. Something is definitely wrong!" It was Sunday afternoon. David was in New York picking Teyon up. He insisted, "Today is not Sunday; there is no way I would miss church. Give me my son!" My mother said that David snatched Teyon away with no shoes. He walked out of the door and left his baby bag. The David I knew would have never done this. He was a good father, and he visited his son every other week. To walk out of the door without diapers or other necessities that the baby needed was uncharacteristic of him, to say the least.

The Devil Introduces Himself to David

One night a really scary event happened. Leilah describes this event, along with my cousin Angie:

It was Sunday evening, and David had come back from picking up Teyon from New York. I was in Syracuse working, so I was not able to be there. I know that people do not want to believe in the things that I am about to share, but what I share really happened. David and I do not hesitate to tell this story at all. The devil is real, and he introduced himself to David's family on this Sunday evening.

Angie had just rededicated her life to the Lord. She told me what happened to David there in his mom's home. She said she looked into David's eyes, and he seemed to "not be there." She told me that she saw the devil in David's eyes.

She said that David started acting like two different persons. His expressions began to change, and Angie could swear that a demon was looking at her behind David's eyes. Angie called her mother, David's Aunt Bert, on the phone and told her, "Ma, I think you need to come over and pray for David. Something is wrong with him." David had left the house when Angie called Aunt Bert, but by the time she arrived David was back.

Aunt Bert was a matriarchal figure in David's family. She lived a consistent life of holiness before the family, and everyone respected her as a woman who knew God well. She came into the house and greeted everyone. She stood up and loudly said with a voice of authority, "Let's pray!"

David immediately jumped up and took over. He told everybody where to stand and made sure that he was totally in charge of what and how they would pray. He even went so far as to tell everyone where to stand based on his judgment of where their relationship with God was.

Angie's story continues in her own words:

Ma got fed up with the spirit that was using David and looked into David's eyes and demanded, "Stop it and sit down, in the name of Jesus!" David stood stiff as a board with a blank look on his face and then obeyed her words, sitting down and looking straight ahead. When she began to lead us in prayer, David slid off of the sofa and started moving across the floor like a snake.

Nobody was ready for what they witnessed that day. David seemed to be in some kind of trance and something had taken over his body. Ma took authority and addressed whatever was inside David that had taken control of him.

She shouted to the spirit in David, "What is your name?"

In a grossly deep voice that was not David's, out of his mouth came words everyone in the room heard: "I am Satan!"

As I mentioned earlier, no one was ready for this. David's mom was not even a Christian at the time. She could not fathom what was going on with her only son. Ma knew what time it was, and she began to yell, looking at David, "Devil, come out of him in the name of Jesus!" Those in the room who did not understand were baffled as to how Ma was yelling at David but seemed to be speaking to someone or something else. It was too far out of our league spiritually for any of us to understand.

Angie has told me that they prayed for me for hours. I seemed to get some relief from this demonic attack, but I still was not acting like the David everyone knew. Angie says that I had a glassy look in my eyes, and everyone in the room knew that the David they knew was no longer there. My mom had been drinking, and I am sure the way I looked and acted must have blown her mind. Angie continues by saying:

As David continued to have episodes of slithering across the floor, his mom jumped on top of his body and looked him in the face, saying, "Son, this is your momma. Do you trust me?" David did not say a word but nodded his head up and down to signal to his mom that he did trust her. Even as he nodded his head up and down, though, it was at a slow and hesitant pace.

As David's mom lay across his body, talking to him to gain his trust, she convinced him that he needed to go to the hospital. By this time, some family members had made calls to David's pastor and some church members. Everyone was praying.

THE PSYCH WARD

Leilah describes what happened when I was taken to the psychiatric ward at East Orange General Hospital:

I flew into New Jersey to see about my man. I was very upset, and my mind could not picture what was being explained to me.

I was not able to see David for the first day. After the staff allowed me to visit him on the second day in the hospital, reality kicked in. David was so happy to see me, but I was not happy to see the person who greeted me. This was not my David! The handsome football player from Montclair that I fell in love with was now the helpless, out-of-control person who sat before me.

I was pregnant and my nerves were shot. David kept sliding off of the bed and going in and out of conversations that did not make sense. I stayed with him all day long, and my eyes could not believe what I saw. Something had taken over David's mind. I really got worried when he started lying on the bed straight as a board. He would look up at the ceiling, pointing at it, never saying a word.

I wondered if I would have to take care of him like this for the rest of his life. It seemed so final because I could not imagine him shaking off this state. Doubts from my nursing experience plagued me. I had dealt with psychiatric patients before, and David definitely was a qualified case.

By this time, my coach was aware I was in the hospital. The player development representative from the Giants came to see me. He stayed with me most of the day, just to observe how I was acting. He asked me questions about what I was hearing and seeing.

Leilah could tell that I was getting frustrated, and although she knew that the man was only doing his job, she could not stand to see me made to look like a fool. I started to have what seemed to be an anxiety attack and loudly demanded that the representative from the team leave my room.

The guy looked into my eyes with a riveting stare. I knew that he was not going to respond to my request for him to leave. He said, "I am not leaving. It is important that I stay here with you." Helpless to do anything about it, I calmed down and did not say anything else.

The team chaplain also came to visit me. He was a very nice man, but even he did not have a real revelation—did not seem to have a clue—about what was going on inside me. Leilah says that the man she loved was in spiritual warfare, and only God could bring me out of it.

Leilah was with me through it all. She continues by telling how the situation worsened:

David's mom did not come to the hospital because she thought that David was just going through a temporary phase. It wasn't until Dave's Aunt Juanita visited David in his hospital room and told her what she had seen that she knew his illness could be worse than what she wanted to admit.

As a nurse, I thought of schizophrenia, which usually manifests in the lives of its sufferers when they are in their midtwenties. David was twenty-four years old, but I refused to think schizophrenia was what we were witnessing. Yet there was obviously something wrong. Dave was having another frantic episode, and I was trying to calm him down when David's Aunt Juanita walked into the room. She freaked out about his condition. She yelled at the top of her voice, "This boy is not all right; he is in trouble!"

Soon the doctor came into the room, and David began to have another outburst. He picked up his aunt's coat and started heading for the door like he was leaving. He was under the impression that his aunt's coat belonged to him. He thought it was time to go.

Then David started sliding off the bed again. He slid across the floor to the window and held his arms out to the side like he was Jesus on the cross. This was too much for me, and I began to lose it. David was clearly out of his mind! I demanded that they sedate him. He had not been to sleep for days and seemed to be delirious, and he refused the pills that were given him.

I kept yelling, "Give him a shot or something. He needs to be sedated! He needs to rest!" All kinds of thoughts were going through my mind. I was pregnant with his child. I did not know if the man that I loved would wake up and not recognize me or his children ever again. Everything was getting worse by the minute.

I became hysterical. I just could not handle what was happening. The Giants' team representative calmed me down and took me to get something to eat.

Later, after things were quiet, the doctor pulled us into the hall to speak about David's condition. He looked at me with a big sigh of relief and said, "Everything is going to be fine. The CT scan showed that he does not have a tumor."

My anger boiled up again. I frowned at the doctor and said, "What do you mean everything is going to be all right because he does not have a tumor? It is not going to be all right until we know what is wrong with him!" I could not believe it. I asked myself, "Is this all we're going to find out?"

My professionalism kicked in, and I told the doctor that, as a nurse, I expected him to tell me what David's problem was. I knew that if we could not diagnose the situation, there could be no remedy. You cannot fix a thing when you do not have an idea of what is wrong. I ran into the bathroom in David's room and really cried out to God for the first time. It was just my first step toward Him, but I knew that this thing was bigger than medical technology or psychological studies. I said a simple prayer: "Lord, I do not know what is wrong with Dave, but can You fix it? You made David, and You are his God. Can You fix it?"

The next day he was scheduled to meet with the staff psychologist. She was a sharp lady and seemed to know what she was doing. I could not help but believe there was something special about her. She evaluated David and gave us an appointment to visit her after he was released.

Finally, David was sedated and got some rest. The voices
that had been speaking to him finally quieted down some.
They were still there, but at least he could rest.

I remained a patient in that hospital for four long days. On my
third day there, God delivered me from the demonic oppression
that I was suffering. I cried out to God, "Father, I do not know
what is going on with me, but I give it all up to You!"

Immediately the voices I had been hearing went completely
away. Without any psychiatric treatment, medicine, or coun-
seling, Jesus set me free! Leilah says that over a period of days,
I gradually, fully came back to myself. I do not remember a lot
of the things that happened to me during those two weeks, but I
do remember that I was suffering from demonic oppression and
God set me free.

Leilah and I learned a lot about demonic oppression in those
days and even more later, when our spiritual mother, Kimberly,
talked to us about a demon that some call "a religious spirit." All
I can remember from the hours before my family committed me
to the hospital is the smell of liquor on my mom's breath. The
religious spirit that had oppressed me could not stand the smell
of the liquor. It was literally tormenting me during that time.

Before that time, I could have never imagined that the devil
would reveal himself in my life by masquerading in the name
of Jesus. But as I read my Bible now, I see that he did it and still
does it all the time.

Leilah saw firsthand the effects of sleep deprivation on someone's spiritual condition. As Pastor Kimberly later pointed out,
lack of sleep plays a big part in a person's physical body being
open to demon manifestation. Once I began to get some rest, the
demonic attacks began to subside.

From Bondage to Freedom

Leilah gives her perspective of this time of great spiritual warfare:

David has never had any other incidents of this sort again. When he told God he was giving his situation over to Him, he really meant it. I have witnessed David's walk with God since that time from a very close position. He is a strong, stable man of God! I can understand why the devil wanted to get him off course when he first met God.

I know that there may be people reading this book who may not understand what we have shared. But it is all truthful, so that's all right.

There are people reading this book who have been living under similar spiritual attacks. They need answers to what is going on.

These answers may not necessarily be through medicine or a medical specialist, but God also works through doctors, nurses, and other health professionals who follow Him. I am a medical professional, and I believe that God anoints people in the field of health care. The staff psychologist at the hospital was a believer. When David did his follow-up appointment with her, she prayed with him. She also told us she had been praying for him while he was in the hospital. I knew there was something special about her even though I did not know that she was a Christian. It was the presence of God in her life.

The discovery of antibiotics was a major breakthrough in the health industry around the world. The important thing to remember is that God anointed the mind of a man to discover penicillin. He also anointed the hands of a man to follow through on what his mind told him that he could do. I have to go further in saying that when situations arise that are out of our hands, God can fix them!

I do not know who or what you believe in, but I pray you believe in someone greater than yourself or in what you can do with your own hands. With all the things we have achieved in time and technology, we are so limited and far behind the mind of God.

David learned who the devil was very early in his walk with God. God was working miracles for David long before the catch at Super Bowl XLII. My prayer is that as you read about his life, you will agree that the miracle God has worked in David's life *is about more than just the catch*!

By the time we were married, David was changing into a new man. The witness in his life made me also give my life to Christ. It has been a growing process from that time up to now. After four years and four children, I am so glad that I endured my fight for love at first sight. David is a wonderful father and a faithful husband. Our testimony is that God delivers! I am the most blessed woman in the world to have a God-fearing man like David Tyree.

FLYING UNDER AND ABOVE THE RADAR

As I read the way my wife tells the story of what I went through my first year in the NFL and with God, I cannot help but be thankful. After all that I have been through, I am not ashamed of any of it, and I have no regrets. When God makes you free…there is no regret needed!

It may seem as though most of my accomplishments have

gone unnoticed in the NFL. As I hear the statements of my peers, many of them say, "David has played under the radar, and his position is one that often goes unnoticed."

My response to this is that I am grateful for all that God has done for me, and I believe that He kept me under the radar for such a time as this. In the Bible, Esther flew under the radar during her first years as queen. Her position was important all the time, though people did not recognize it.

When the time came and it counted the most, Esther flew above the radar so that God could reveal His purpose through her. Her actions not only saved many lives but also spared an entire nation.

Though Esther was a woman, the spiritual principle applies to both women and men. God's purpose kept me under the radar until the time He planned for me to rise above it. Everything happened just as God planned it. God was watching over my situation the whole time, and He knew what would happen at the Super Bowl before I signed my contract with the New York Giants.

Even my status as an "under-the-radar player" is God's mighty plan. When I think of how close I came to destroying my career and even myself, I realize that I could have been dismissed from the NFL my rookie year. What happened at the "Supernatural Bowl" didn't happen because of the actions of a superstar. If a superstar player would have made that play with Eli, there would have been less hype about it, the players would have received all the credit, and God would not have received the glory. God used a "nobody" in the eyes of people to accomplish His plan. This is the great thing about flying under God's radar—when He gets ready to promote you, no one can take the credit from Him. Men will say, "Only God!"

Please do not think I am in any way complaining against those whom God chooses to put in the limelight. He uses all kinds of situations for His purposes. I just feel sorry for those who never get the revelation of Psalm 75:6–7. It says: "For exaltation comes neither from the east nor from the west nor from the south. But God is the Judge: He puts down one, and exalts another."

So many people fail to recognize when they have been gloriously set up by God. To those of you who are reading this book and feel like you have been doing great things under the radar but that no one has noticed, be encouraged! Hebrews 12:1 says that we are surrounded by a great cloud of witnesses in heaven. They see everything that goes on in the earth. What you do with a good heart and right motives never goes unnoticed.

I believe that there will be an awards ceremony in heaven that the Oscars, the Grammy Awards, the Hall of Fame, and any other great institutions of recognition cannot touch. I thank God for every accomplishment I have been recognized for in this life. Despite this, I cannot help but look forward to being at that rewards ceremony in heaven. I plan on sitting next to my mother in glory.

HUSBAND, FATHER, AND ROLE MODEL

God brought me out of alcohol and women, but He did more than that: He brought me out of the bondage of the enemy. I have the type of testimony that some people can't relate to. They can't handle me saying that demons were talking to me. But it's a reality. The supernatural realm is more real than the natural.

We have to believe that if we also believe that God is real. I knew from experience that God was real, and I knew He was faithful. I began to tell my boys and my teammates what had happened to me and how God stood by me.

Some of the guys looked at me like, "Who are you? Weed man turned preacher now!" I still get those sideways looks sometimes. I hope I've shown the guys that my new life in Christ is more than just another temporary high.

Since those days in 2004 when God confronted me with how much I needed Him, I have settled down to be the husband to Leilah that I hadn't been before God took hold of me. We are active in a Christian fellowship, and I also try to participate in organizations that allow me to speak to students about the dangers of drugs. I also want to get across to kids the importance of academic excellence, and I've spoken to my high school in Montclair, New Jersey, among others, to encourage the students there to excel. It is important to me to be a role model to kids who are going through issues and situations that are similar to those I went through. I came out on the other side, and they can too through the grace of God. I'll share that message any chance I get!

I'm not much of a golfer, but I can throw balls, most of them, anyway, down a lane at a bowling alley. I started a David Tyree All-Pro Bowling Classic in 2006, which benefits the International Children's Fund (ICF). ICF raises funds to support charities that assist the needs of underprivileged youth, children with special needs and medical needs, and children living in third world countries.

Leilah and I started our Next in Line program in 2006, a ministry to youth from the ages of eleven to eighteen. This ministry is designed to pour into and reach the hearts of young people with hopes of raising up warriors for Christ. We desire for them to understand that God is not about regimens, rules, and regulations, but He is all about *relationships*. There is freedom that comes in being a child of God, but that identity can only be found in Christ. We will be sending kids to camp and providing other educational and life experiences to promote strong character.

Nine

A BITTERSWEET SEASON

*And we know that all things work together
for good to those who love God, to those who
are the called according to His purpose.*

—ROMANS 8:28

On December 15, 2007, I was called out of a team meeting. As soon as I saw the expression on my wife's face, I knew that something was seriously wrong.

Words came out of her mouth, but when I heard them, my mind seemed to shut down. I heard what she said, but it simply did not compute. "Your mother had a massive heart attack, and she did not make it through."

I turned to the window. "She was not even sick!" I repeated this to myself over and over. My mind tried to convince me that my wife's words were not true. It took a while for reality to set in.

What had happened? Where was she when it had happened? Who was with her? All of these questions crowded into my thoughts about my mom.

I began to break down and release the sorrow. I sat down in a chair, and in the midst of tears I began to praise and worship

God because I felt it had to be His will. As I was collecting my thoughts and trying to get myself together, I felt a hand touch me on my back, and I heard a voice say, "Son, everything is going to be all right."

The voice came from Coach Tom Coughlin. When I saw who it was, it caught me off guard. His words were comforting, and boy, did I need to hear some words of comfort. I thought the voice sounded like the voice of God, and I almost laughed! The support from my coaches and teammates was tremendous. Many prayed with me right there, and others gave me their heartfelt condolences. The love I felt from them added to the love of my family that surrounded me as I thought of what my mom meant to me.

Thelma Tyree had always been my best friend. She was a mild-mannered woman and very pleasant to be around. A few years ago she moved to Lake City, Florida, where my oldest sister had purchased land. I visited her as often as I could during the off-season, and we always had great times together in Florida. My mother's favorite way to spend time was watching ESPN with her cat, Mickey. She watched the Olympics, the NBA playoffs, and the Super Bowl with that cat in her lap.

Mickey had been a gift to her from her best friend, Evangelist Tia. If you wanted to get on my mom's bad side, all you had to do was say something about her cat. She would say, "If you got a problem with Mickey, you got a problem with Thelma." Most of us were allergic to the cat. This was an issue for us, but we dared not let my mother know! She treated Mickey like a human being. He slept with her in the bed every night. Whenever my mom went on trips away from home, she would drive for hours to get back in time to take care of her Mickey.

I gave my life to the Lord before my mother did. I was a brand-new Christian and had a false zeal that made me try to push Jesus down her throat. I even had the nerve to tell my mom once, "If you do not get saved, you're going to hell." Thank God that by His mercy and grace my mother still came to know in a personal way the Creator of the universe!

Despite my religious ignorance, our relationship remained tight. My mother attended almost every one of my home games before she moved to Florida. She never mentioned having a favorite football team, but I knew that her team was the team that I was on at the time.

When I visited Syracuse University years before to check into its football scholarship offer, I was so happy that my mother went with me. By the time I was in the tenth grade, I started receiving recruitment letters from major universities. In my junior year, getting a scholarship became a reality.

I did not have a struggle choosing Syracuse. So many things pointed in that direction. First of all, it was a Division IA school. Philadelphia Eagles quarterback Donovan McNabb had had a successful career at Syracuse, which also won the Big East championship during the months I was being recruited to play there. The program at Syracuse was also known for preparing young men for more than the NFL. They prepared their athletes for life. Syracuse was highlighted for having a high percentage of athletes receiving college degrees. I was proud to be the first in my family to attend a major university, and one with a very good reputation. But in spite of everything else stacked in SU's favor, Mom was truly the reason I chose SU. The smile on her face as we sat in the meeting with the head coach was priceless.

My last years of high school were some of the happiest times of my mother's life. As a single mother, sending a child off to college was a great joy for her. A scholarship offer made it even greater. From the games at Syracuse through my years with the New York Giants, my mother supported me wholeheartedly. Sometimes she had such a big smile on her face I could not see the corners of her mouth from the front.

I did not have a lot of hope for being drafted into the NFL. My mother, father, and I were lying around in the living room watching the draft on television. I was dozing off during the program. The phone actually rang and woke us up. My mother answered the phone and whispered to me, "It's the New York Giants." I wanted to scream. Not only was I drafted, but I would also be playing in my hometown! I will never forget the huge smile on her face.

My mother always lived a very simple life. When she moved to Florida, she did not have a strong relationship with the Lord. She was not a churchgoing person, and she was still drinking, cursing, and smoking a little marijuana. She would say, "Let the Lord deal with me in my way." She had always talked about the Lord and respected the things of God, but she was not a religious person. My mother was just *real*. My sisters and I had also smoked marijuana in the house. We never smoked with my mother, but we knew that she smoked, and vice versa.

Then in Florida, Mom met a young evangelist named Tia. Tia was my oldest sister's best friend, and they attended college together in Tallahassee at Florida A&M University. Tia knew that my mother had some issues that needed to be dealt with in her life, but she never judged her. They just "took" to each other. Tia had lost her mother when she was young, while at the same time my mom needed spiritual guidance. She would say to my mother, "You be my mother, and I will be your evangelist."

Tia was a virgin until she married her husband two years ago at the age of thirty-three. My mother taught her things that a new bride needed to know, and Tia taught my mother things that a new creature in Christ needed to know. The relationship was heaven-sent. My mother began traveling on the road with Tia as her assistant. She did not immediately get rid of her habits, though, and one day Tia walked into a room where my mother was smoking marijuana.

My mom looked into Tia's eyes and confessed with a convicted heart, "I am so sorry you had to see this."

From that day forward my mother never smoked another joint. She told Tia, "I am going to sell out to God and do this road thing with you, for Jesus." My mother began to grow in the things of God, and we could see the fruit of Tia's labor. She joined Miracle Tabernacle Church, and Apostle Cleopatra Steele became her pastor. From that point on, Mom was surrounded by strong people of God.

I finally got to talk to Tia on that day in December. Still shocked about what happened, Tia attempted to explain everything to me in detail. My mother had gone to a conference in West Palm Beach with Tia. Tia was the speaker, and the theme of the meeting was "Liberated Woman." This meeting had touched my mom's life in such a way that she could not stop talking about it.

Tia said that my mom kept saying, "Tia, I am a liberated woman!" My mom had tried to call my sisters and me to let us know about what had happened at the meeting. She wanted to share this newfound liberation in Jesus that she had received.

I spoke to my mother earlier that day when she had called

about Teyon's birthday party. It seemed like any other time when I spoke with my mom. Our conversation had been very brief. Little did I know it would be the last time I would hear my mom's voice.

Tia went on to tell me more about what happened right after the meeting in West Palm Beach. They drove to Tia's house, and my mom went to rest on her bed. She asked Tia to bring Tia's small son Jaylen to her, saying, "We are going to chill out together." Tia thought it was a little strange for my mom to ask that because my mom did not spend a lot of time with children.

Tia gave the child to my mom and stepped away from the room. Seconds later Tia said that she heard a gurgling sound. As she went back into the room, my mom was lying on the bed choking, with the child next to her. As she struggled to breathe, she tried to say, "I'm liberated—I'm liberated." Tia attempted to do CPR on my mom, but with her last breath Mom declared, "I'm liberated!" She closed her eyes and slipped into glory.

My mom never got a chance to call us and tell us about her liberating experience, but we got the message. As much as it hurt—we got the message! As I remember her now, I realize that she sensed that she would be with the Lord soon.

My mother was a poet, and her dream of publishing a book came to pass when she released a collection of poetry called *Soul Articulation*. She wrote a poem only one week before her death that I am honored to share now:

GOD HAS THE ANSWER
by Thelma Tyree

Only God has the answer
To birth as well as death.

He knew my end from my beginning
Before I drew my first breath.
He knew me in the womb
Before I was swaddled in clothes;
He had my story destined
Before my book was closed.
He has the pages written
And sealed before the dream
My parents had me in mind
While I was still a gleam.
Although no one could know
It would end like this;
Every well-written story
Has an unexpected twist.
As long as there is a chapter
That tells how one fine day
My soul met with Jesus
As I traveled in my way.
I heard His word and received Him
As my salvation and light;
So my reward is glory
Now, I can reap eternal life;
The Master and Ruler of our fates
Has restored us to the Father.
The tears you shed are tears of joy
As He receives me in His glory.
Life is the – [dash] that happens
Between birth and death;
Only God has the answer
Before I drew my first breath.

My mother's poem shows she knew in her spirit that her time was near, even though her mind did not have a clue. Reading it after her death was a bittersweet moment. I miss my mom dearly, but at the same time I know that she is at her final destination in glory. My mother died at the young age of only fifty-nine. It was early, but it was not a tragedy. It was shocking and sad, but it was not a time of gloom and doom. She really is a liberated woman! She has received the greatest level of liberation a human can receive, to be absent from the body and present with the Lord.

We had a memorial service for my mother at her church in Florida. Afterward, we flew her body back to New Jersey for her home-going service. We put my mother away really nice because she deserved it. She was royalty! The service was held at my church, and Bishop Charles Harris Jr. did the eulogy. I was filled with mixed emotions as a horse and carriage pulled my mother's body through the streets from the church to the cemetery.

The highlight of the service for me was the reading at the funeral of a poem that my cousin Rachael had written. Years ago my cousin had a near-death experience. She had gone to heaven and hell. After my mom died, the Lord allowed her to see my mother in heaven in a dream. She has always had spiritual encounters of this sort.

It brought such joy to my heart to hear Rachael testify about the dream. She said she saw my mother dancing and praising the Lord in heaven. My cousin said that my mom was happy and did not want to come back.

God is so good to share that vision with my family. So many people lose loved ones and have an emptiness in their heart concerning their fate. Though I miss my mom, my heart is at peace. I know she wants us to keep her in our hearts and to live our lives. My comfort is to live my life in a way that I will one day see her in heaven.

Here is the poem Rachael dedicated to her aunt, Thelma
Tyree:

In my dreams, Father, I begged, just let me meet You by
the tree
You know the place, God, where You once took me
And before first morning dew, You answered so
graciously
Allowed me to see You again as I requested of Thee
In what seemed like less than a blink of an eye
Just like that You appeared; a lovely vision in white.
I couldn't move 'n couldn't speak for behold a brand-new
creation
And oh what a spectacular sight
Can hardly believe my eyes; my teardrops are as rain
I want to run to You, hold You, tell you I love You again
Please, Lord, can I? just one more time?
Like a whisper in the gentle breeze that rustles through
the leaves
The still small voice echoed like a soothing chime
Through the windows I have allowed you to see; I have
given you a glance,
Know I am with her, child, and she is with Me
Fret not, for one day you too will have your chance
Your hair is radiant platinum, each strand was a glow
With the glory of the Lord as if you had on a halo
As I gazed upon a beauty I had never seen before
I noticed light coming from your garment and its lumi-
nescent sheen
A long heavenly white raiment with real gold embel-
lished trim
That glistened on each sleeve end and had even more
gold at the hem

Moving left to right as you glide, your gown gave such a
fiery glare
Swaying back and forth with every wave of each arm
I watched you make circle round about this tree
Fields of lavender behind you full of perfume so sweet
Blissfully and gracefully you danced with your hands
lifted high
Wonder if you can see me, do you know I cannot stay,
I'm only here to say good-bye?
Then you dropped your hands a li'l lower, wriggled them
around
And with that very special jingling of the bracelet
I knew I had my answer just by that precious sound
I saw the most wide and beautiful smile across your
face
As if to say, "Yes, I've finally made my final residence"
This wonderful beautiful glorious place!
You knelt down by the tree and ran your fingers through
the flowers
That had been rejoicing all along
Waiting in expectancy, bursting with color and
excitement
Ready to sing you a new song.
We're so happy that you've arrived because we've been
waiting here for so long
To have our angel back with us, in the arms of Jesus
where you belong
No more worry, not a care, no more sickness or despair
No more heartache, no more pain, no more stress and
no more strain
Welcome to the tree where there is no strife
Come dwell at the tree—this is the tree of life.
So, I will see you later, I know this is not the end
Where your old life has ended, your real life now begins

A newly decorated home is ready, your chariot awaits!!!
One day I'll meet you by the tree, beyond the pearly
gates
I will meet you there by the tree, auntie, beyond the
pearly gates.

My mother's death was so unexpected and happened so fast
that my sisters Tara and Jessica and I did not have time to even
think about the plans we had already made. Tara, the oldest,
was building a home on the property next to my mom's mobile
home in Florida. I was also about to purchase land in the area.
We hoped to spend more time together as a family, but God had
another plan.

I think my mother's death took its hardest toll on Tara. She
was really looking forward to being close to our mom. She had
left home to join the marines at the age of seventeen and had
never lived at home again. She and her husband presently pastor
a church in Alabama, but they will go ahead and move to the
new house in Lake City as they had planned.

Overall, my mom's death has drawn all of us closer together,
and we have embraced the fact that she is with the Lord. I really
missed seeing her smiling face at the Super Bowl game, but I
know she watched it from a VIP seat in heaven. I felt her presence
in my heart because I knew that she would have never
missed that game.

I pray that you and your loved ones will also draw closer
together as you read my story.

———

Oh, yeah—I bet you're wondering what happened to my mother's
spoiled cat, Mickey. Mickey was the only living thing that I had

to remember my mother by. We took Mickey to New Jersey, but my children were allergic to him. He had to stay in the basement of the house most of the time. We could tell that Mickey missed my mom. He seemed like such a sad cat after she died. One day, my spiritual mom, Kimberly, came over, and the cat immediately took to her. Though she had never liked cats, she thought that this cat was special. She knew how much Mickey meant to my sisters and me, so she took him to her house, planning to find him a good home.

Mickey never left Kimberly's house, and now he is more spoiled than ever! Mickey sleeps in the bed with her every night. She says that Mickey gets up every morning with her to pray just as he did with my mom. He is her Commander of the Morning mascot. (I'll explain what a Commander of the Morning is in a later chapter.) I know my mom in heaven is smiling at Kimberly and Mickey praying together.

Ten

FROM WILD CARD TO WINNER

Rutherford, New Jersey, late summer 2007. My expectation for the 2007 football season was high. I had a good, steady training camp. Nothing spectacular happened. My goal was to be at least third on the depth chart for wide receivers. Overall, our team seemed to be stronger than ever before. We were coming toward the end of training camp and almost down to our fifty-three-player roster. The pressure of making an NFL team is unimaginable. Every player at camp is good, or he would not be there. The odds of making it into the league are so low they're hard to even calculate. Two key things have helped me through training camps over the past years:

1. Performing when it counts
2. Wanting it most

Focusing on these keys has kept me from being distracted with excessive pressure.

As the season began, the pressure was not just on the players to make the team. Negative rumors were spreading like wildfire. It did not make things better when team captain Michael Strahan did not show up for training camp. Everyone was murmuring about his contractual issues with the team management. Would he be back this year? The question floated in the air and in the media. The press seemed to feed off of the issues that concerned our team, and controversy lingered over our heads like a dark cloud. Though our team was strong on the field, something was still missing—something was just not right. Our entire team was under pressure. Both Coach Tom Coughlin and Eli Manning, our starting quarterback, were under attack. We lost the first two games of the season, and our defense had given up eighty points during these games. We could hear the fans in the stands yelling, "Get rid of the quarterback!" or "We need a new coach!"

I thank God that Coach Coughlin identified the missing link. He spearheaded the fact that we needed stronger relationship ties on the team. He admitted to the team and before the press, "I just need to do things differently." We needed a bridge built between Coach Coughlin and the players. There was a communication gap there. We also needed more unity among the players.

Coach Coughlin did not just identify the problem; he did something about it. He implemented a leadership committee that consisted of five offensive and five defensive veteran players. These players met with Coach Coughlin to discuss issues concerning the players and the coaches. The ten players chosen acted as mediators between the players and Coach Coughlin. He gave the leadership committee his expectations, and they relayed them to the team. This committee also relayed the players' concerns back to Coach Coughlin. All communication gaps were closed, and everyone knew what was expected of them. There was no room for excuses.

Coach Coughlin's plan changed the atmosphere within our team. A closeness that I had never witnessed over the years manifested itself on and off of the field. Better player-to-player and coach-to-player relationships were created. Everyone noticed the difference, and we liked it. The guys on the team were hanging out with each other after work. The great thing about the change was that we did not have to deal with any superegos.

The 2006 season was disappointing—a player even verbally bashed Coach Coughlin and Eli Manning on national television. There was none of that in the 2007 season. It was all about the team, and we could feel the power of our unity. We did not have any ball hogs on our offensive lineup, and the defensive linemen worked together like one big wall that did not give an opposing quarterback a chance.

Coach Coughlin's appointed council of players also dealt with novice athletes and the problems they had with their discipline and performance requirements. The veteran players imparted wisdom into the younger players, and the entire team seemed to be on point. The leaders were leading, and the ones who were supposed to follow were following. The results were that fewer players got in trouble with discipline issues and infractions of the law. We also got to know a Coach Coughlin that we had not seen before. Everyone noticed how he began to deal with us differently. The change was for the good.

A world championship cannot be won without teamwork. The word that comes to my mind when I think of teamwork is *selflessness*. Selflessness requires a person to lay aside his own agenda to submit to the greater good of what he is involved in. Real teamwork shows itself when every team member does his part. Each one must have the overall vision and the tenacity to press into the goal. We began to experience this selflessness among us as the weeks went by. We finally played as one—one team on the way to victory.

THE ROAD TO VICTORY

With a regular season record of 10-6, we were on our way to the wild-card play-off game. Up to this point our team did not stand out as having championship potential. On January 6 we defeated the Tampa Bay Buccaneers 24-14 for the wild-card slot. Though we were not considered a threat as a team, we were on our way to the divisional round of the play-offs. Most people probably thought we would be knocked out in the first round.

On January 13 we played the team known as "America's Team," the Dallas Cowboys. We defeated the Cowboys 21-17. People were a little moved by this victory, but not too much. They did not know if the win was chance or luck.

I don't think it was either. I knew that we were on the road to victory. I cannot explain it; I just felt it in my bones.

Every victory we experienced in the play-offs put more gas in our tanks. We moved down this road with more tenacity. Our confidence grew, and we became even closer as a team. The next game on the schedule was the NFC Championship Game.

We were scheduled to play the Green Bay Packers, at Green Bay, in the heart of the winter season. Who could stand against Green Bay in freezing weather with the most zealous fans in the league cheering the Packers on? It also did not help that they had one of the best quarterbacks in the NFL. Who could imagine a victory for the Giants? The answer to this question is easy: We could...the 2007 New York Giants!

The coin was flipped, and the game was on. I cannot remember ever being so cold in my life—I heard it went down to -23° F that day. We had to focus on playing the game and avoiding frostbite at the same time. The Packers were a little more accustomed to this weather, and they had the home-team advantage.

Reggie Anderson Photography

David Tyree

Eighth-grade graduation trip to Hersheypark, PA

Leilah and David, summer of 2001. Yes, I still had hair!

David and Mom after spring game, April 1999

*(Left to right) Keeon Walker (roommate), Chris Davis,
Maurice McClain (roommate), and David. Best friends at college*

Tribute to favorite rapper at the time, Jim Jones, 2004

*Mom (Thelma Tyree), David, and Dad (Jesse Tyree Jr.)
at Syracuse University Commencement, May 2002*

David and Leilah on their wedding day

David, Leilah, and Teyon

Coach Tom Coughlin and David at 2005 Kickoff Luncheon, receiving 2004 Special Teams

*(Left to right) Eli Manning, Osi Umenyiora, David, Tiki Barber,
and Coach Tom Coughlin, 2005 Kickoff Luncheon*

New York Giants quarterback Eli Manning (10) and receiver David Tyree (85) celebrate Tyree's touchdown in the fourth quarter during the Super Bowl XLII football game against the New England Patriots at University of Phoenix Stadium on Sunday, February 3, 2008, in Glendale, Arizona.

New York Giants David Tyree celebrates his touchdown during the fourth quarter of the NFL's Super Bowl XLII football game against the New England Patriots in Glendale, Arizona, February 3, 2008.

New York Giants receiver David Tyree celebrates his touchdown against the New England Patriots in the second half of Super Bowl XLII at University of Phoenix Stadium in Glendale, Arizona, on Sunday, February 3, 2008.

New York Giants receiver David Tyree (85) pulls in a 32-yard pass as New England Patriots safety Rodney Harrison (37) tries to defend during the fourth quarter of the Super Bowl football game Sunday, February 3, 2008, in Glendale, Arizona. The Giants won 17-14.

New York Giants receiver David Tyree (85) holds on by his fingertips to a 32-yard pass as New England Patriots safety Rodney Harrison (37) pulls him down after the catch during the fourth quarter of the Super Bowl XLII football game at University of Phoenix Stadium on Sunday, February 3, 2008, in Glendale, Arizona.

New York Giants' David Tyree reenacts his fourth-quarter catch at a celebration rally Tuesday, February 5, 2008, at Giants Stadium in East Rutherford, New Jersey. The New York Giants beat the New England Patriots 17-14 in Super Bowl XLII.

2008 Super Bowl XLII Ring Ceremony. (Left to right) Master of Ceremonies
Bob Pappa, Coach Tom Coughllin, and David

Godfather, Leroy Bowers, and David after the ticker-tape
parade in New York City, 2008, with the Lombardi Trophy

Tara Williams, David, and Jessica Noel—my older, little sisters.

Spiritual Mom, Kim Daniels, and David, all smiles

Daddy and his boys, Teyon and Josiah

Extended family, (left to right) Tara Williams holding Sophia, Leilah, David and Josiah, Kim Daniels, Teyon, and Jessica holding Hannah

Leilah, Teyon, David, and Josiah. Hannah and Sophia are only two weeks away.

David with Leilah, Sophia, and Hannah, the women of my life

We controlled the field the entire time. After missing what some would call two "must-have" field goals to win the game, Lawrence Tynes kicked a 47-yard field goal in overtime to send the New York Giants into Super Bowl XLII. Considering the conditions and what was at stake, the field goal was nothing short of a miracle. The team was on fire! I have never seen such a fired-up group of guys! We had become the 2007 NFC champions in the most competitive division in the league!

I could hear the players yelling at the top of their voices in the locker room, "We did it, we did it!" "Yeah!"

We played a great game, but with my fists clenched tight I added in a low but strong voice, "God did it!"

We were on our way to Phoenix, Arizona, to play in the Super Bowl! The hype amongst the players at this point was unimaginable. We had accomplished the impossible by winning seven regular season games and three post-season games on the road. The road behind us was long, and the road in front of us was getting shorter every day. In one more game we could end up as world champions.

We were the underdogs, of course, and the world was betting against us. But I thought, if God is for us, who can be against us? In my mind nothing could stop us now. We had come too far, and we refused to die hard. Defeat was not an option, and failure was not the plan! Personally speaking, I could taste the victory, and I am sure that my teammates felt the same way.

Because of our burst of last-minute victories, we were launched from mediocrity to the limelight. So many records were about to be made or broken. It was not about where we were but how far we had come. We had come down a long road, and it felt great!

These were the records that were at hand:

- We had become the ninth wild-card team in NFL history to reach the Super Bowl and could be named the fifth wild-card team to win it.
- Seated fifth in the play-offs, we would become the lowest-seated NFC team in NFL history to win the Super Bowl.
- We would also become the third team in history to win the Super Bowl after starting a season with a 0-2 record.
- It would also become a never forgotten, history-making moment to beat the New England Patriots and break their 18-0 rally, stopping them from making NFL history and beating the Miami Dolphins' record of being the only team to have an undefeated season.
- With eleven rookies on our active roster, this would be a record for a Super Bowl championship team.

Our name was being highlighted in the media: "The New York Giants have done it again!" We had a winning streak that could not be broken.

Our team has played in three championships in the history of the organization. Two of those games were won, and one was lost. This year our goal was to put another notch on the winning side. Not even Bill Belichick and his record-breaking team could stop us. Only three words could describe how we felt as a team: Victory is ours!

From the Big Apple to the Valley of the Sun

I woke up every morning after the Green Bay game saying, "It's really true…we are going to the Super Bowl!" I could hardly sleep at night as we prepared to go to Phoenix. The possibility of being the next NFL champions became more of a reality. It was like a dream come true!

Our team management provided great support to ensure that our family members could attend the game. They chartered a plane for all of our family members to fly to Arizona, and they arranged rental cars for the players and set aside a hotel just for our families.

The details were in place so that we only had to focus on bringing those rings back to New York City. The only thing that was different was that I felt as if I was walking around in a dream. I thought I would wake up and tell my wife that I dreamed we made it to the Super Bowl.

As game day grew closer, we practiced and had meetings as usual. We were using the weight room in the Arizona Cardinals' facilities. We lifted a little and got "swole" a little, but none of us went for a hard lift. The biggest preparation was more mental and emotional: being around the guys, vibing off one another, sensing everyone's urgency to win, and enjoying the moments. Most of us also tried to spend time with our families.

Another honor for me was when Arizona Cardinals quarter-back Kurt Warner, a man of great faith, stopped and watched our practice one day. He had been playing for the Giants about the time I decided to follow Christ. I got a chance to thank him for the example he had been to me.

Finally, it was less than twenty-four hours until we would join the ranks of other teams that had made it this far. Going to the

Super Bowl was in itself such an honor. The atmosphere was electric with great expectation. Though the world saw us as the underdogs, we stepped onto the dry desert soil as champions. As I looked into the eyes of my teammates, I could see their hunger for victory. The theme of the Super Bowl was, "Who wants it more?" Every time I saw that advertisement, there was no doubt in my mind, and I yelled, "We do!" as I hit my chest.

The big day was nearly here—and we were ready for it!

Eleven

THE SUPERNATURAL BOWL

P atriots 14, Giants 10. One minute and fifteen seconds
left on the clock at University of Phoenix Stadium in
Glendale, Arizona.

More than 72,000 people were on their feet. Screaming Patriots
fans were already celebrating nonstop. They were sure that the
Pats were going to cap off an undefeated season with the Super
Bowl XLII win.

"Eli, Eli, Eli, Eli," chanted the New York Giants fans. As a
Patriots win seemed to be in the bag, Manning avoided a sack.
He lobbed the ball on a long pass, 32 yards, as more than 143
million people watched the game worldwide.

And then an obscure special teams player jumped up, reached
into the heavens, caught the ball, and mashed it against his
helmet—and held on to it. Pass complete! Within seconds Plaxico
Burress took Manning's next pass, 13 yards, over the goal line
and the New York Giants won the game! "17–14" flashed from the
scoreboard around the world, and "the catch," "the circus grab,"
or "the miracle of the Supernatural Bowl," as I call it, became
Super Bowl history.

That stretch was in more ways than one a high point in my
story, but it lasted only a few seconds. The story that brought me
to that field in February 2008 is twenty-eight years long.

113

Memories of Mom

As the days wound up faster and faster toward Phoenix, I kept thinking about my mom's smile, the one that was so big that it spread across her whole face—that smile that I had been blessed to receive from her so many times. During the week of the Super Bowl I had so many memories of my mother. They were running through my head like a filmstrip. Most of my family attended the game, and we missed her, but no one opened their mouth to mention it. We just kept her in our hearts. It was like a type of silent agreement.

My mind was filled with thoughts of how nice it would have been to have my mother at the game. The only resolve that I had was that God was in charge. Despite this, I was experiencing a bittersweet moment. I was in the midst of a dream come true and one I wished she could have shared with me. To have such a great moment and not have my mother was like putting a negative and a positive wire together. Having Jesus in my heart gave me comfort that she was close to me.

I had always dreamed of one day having a big breakthrough in my football career and doing Campbell's soup commercials with my mom. I just knew that she would be a great Campbell's soup mom! Her smile would have lit up the set. Thoughts like these were going through my mind as I prepared for the game. Tears welled up in my eyes during times when I was off to myself.

Spiritual Preparation

The night before the game I called my spiritual mom and her husband to pray with me, as we had done many times before. They also began to pray for Leilah, who was eight months pregnant with twins. After praying for the babies, Kimberly turned the prayer focus toward my performance at the game. She told me that the Lord showed her a vision of "spiritual glue" on my hands and that she was confident God would give me "the big play." She also said that in her vision my feet looked like an animal's feet (in the Spirit).

She spoke out very loud as if she was surprised, "David, you have hinds' feet, and God is about to quicken you to run!"

Her husband, Ardell, or "Danny" as many people call him, told me the Lord showed him that He was bringing me out of the obscurity of being a special teams player. He said that I would be known as a great wide receiver and the world would know my name.

The words that came to me in prayer that night were great confirmations of what had been said to me before. My accountant, Hubie Synn, called me one day not long before. He did not know me that well, so he seemed hesitant to say what he wanted to say. Despite this, he told me that God was about to highlight my skills as a wide receiver. He said that God was bringing me out of obscurity and that my name was going before me. He also said that God knew my desire to share my faith and that He was giving me a platform to do so. My pastor and spiritual father, Bishop Charles Harris, who has been praying for my family and career for years, also confirmed God's plan for great things about to come.

All of the words spoken to me the night before the game gave confidence to my heart. The Bible says that things will be confirmed by two or three witnesses. God used many more than two or three to confirm what was about to happen at Super Bowl XLII. I heard these words and believed them...

...But I could have never imagined in my greatest dreams what God was actually about to do.

February 3

I awoke the morning of the big game with nervousness in my stomach but a big smile in my heart. Win or no win, even the experience of playing in the Super Bowl was a memorable and honorable moment. The day of the Super Bowl seemed like the longest day of my life. The hands on the clock could not move fast enough! I kept looking around, saying, "What time is it?" I could feel the electricity in the air.

Finally we boarded the bus for the stadium. It was time! Everything I had played, prayed, and practiced was stirring on the inside of me and reaching out for victory. After all the years of wondering what it would be like to play in the Super Bowl, my opportunity to know had finally come. I could experience this moment with fifty-two great guys and an awesome coaching staff and management. Even Coach Coughlin had a look in his eyes that gave no room to defeat. He gave us a visual picture of what it's like to win a championship. Then he proclaimed, "This game is ours!" Everything in me agreed.

The most exciting part of any football game for me is the introduction of the teams. It seemed as though everything stood still and focused on us as we ran through the tunnel onto the field, cleats laced and ready to go. Then local Glendale resident and *American Idol* winner Jordin Sparks sang the national anthem, the coin was flipped, and it was on!

I was standing in the middle of my promise from God. The prayers, prophecies, and words of encouragement were rooted in my spirit while the plays of the game were in my mind.

At the moment of the first kickoff, the thousands of flickering lights from the flashing of cameras nearly blinded me. I could see fans sitting on the edge of their seats. From what I could tell, they didn't move from that position the entire time.

The game was a low-scoring game in the first half. As Ryan Seacrest announced the halftime show featuring Tom Petty and the Heartbreakers, we went into the locker room with a score of 7-3, Patriots leading. Being behind did not make our spirits low. We leaned on the fact that we had come so close to beating the Patriots in an earlier game.

I walked into the locker room amidst a focused and collected team and yelled, "We got this, fellas!" (It was a long halftime, so the locker room was more focused than pumped up.) Michael Strahan commenced to pumping the team up. Our locker room was on fire! There was not an ounce of doubt in the room. If the Patriots were going to beat us, they should have already done it. They had taken too long to make a move because we were too hungry to win. Many people thought that the Patriots were invincible. We knew we had the team to break their winning streak before the world because we were also on a winning streak. Because our destinies had collided in Phoenix, somebody had to stop winning, and we were determined that it would not be us.

I was ready to play in the second half because I knew that the play I had been waiting on for five weeks could possibly be called. I had a horrible practice on the Friday before the game and dropped almost every ball. I went over to Eli to let him know that I was ready. I told myself, "Friday was Friday, but this is Super Bowl Sunday," and I wanted to say the same thing to him. Before I was able to finish my statement, Eli cut me off and looked into my eyes and said, "I know you're ready. I trust you."

It was time to play football. The moment that I had been waiting on had come. The ball was snapped, and I was in the end zone. Eli threw the ball to me, and the play was picture perfect. The ball came to me like I was a magnet and it was a piece of metal. As it dropped into my hands, time seemed to stand still for a minute. When my mind caught up with time, I heard the announcer saying, "Touchdown! David Tyree, number 85!"

It was unbelievable! I made the first touchdown of the game for our team. This was too much for me to take at one time. The feeling was overwhelming. With no touchdowns under my belt all year, the Lord used me to put my team in the lead with a score of 10-7. It was the greatest moment of my football career. My touchdown was the big play that my spiritual mother spoke about, I thought. This reminded me of the scripture in Ephesians 3:20 that says God will do more than our mind can imagine. God has done what He promised through the people who prayed for me and encouraged me!

We all knew, though, that this was not the time to have a victory party. Our feelings were confirmed when the Patriots scored another touchdown with approximately two minutes left in the game. We needed a supernatural drive!

Patriots fans began to celebrate what they thought was a sure victory as we began our drive down the field. I knew that the way things were going we were not driving on our own power. It was really supernatural, and even then it seemed like angels were on the football field working on our behalf. To borrow some words from the Bible, the land was being subdued, and the earth was yielding the increase! Interceptions that should have taken place against us did not happen, and plays that did not make sense kept happening. Everyone from superstars on down to rookies made outstanding plays.

With only a few minutes left to drive toward the goal line and my career at an all-time high, something crazy happened!

Eli Manning was about to throw a pass but was bombarded by defensive linemen. They clearly should have sacked him, but he shook off every sack attempt. It was as if he had oil on his jersey—he kept slipping right through the hands of the Patriot defensive players. Off balance and without time to think, with one minute and fifteen seconds left on the clock, he flung a 32-yard pass in my direction.

I was defended by one of the best and most aggressive safeties ever to play the game, Rodney Harrison. If I missed this ball, our team may not have time to recover. The game would be over. Everyone was depending on me, and I could not let them down. All I could think was, "By any means necessary!" Rodney and I struggled to get the ball as I tried to catch it at its highest point. Only a few seconds went by, but in my mind the play seemed to be running in slow motion as I reached up and behind my head to get the catch. Touching the ball with my fingers and pinning it down to my helmet, I was determined to hold on. I could not let it go! With Rodney on me like a Siamese twin, I hit the ground with my back arched in an awkward position. I was tied in a knot with my defender, but *I still had the ball*. It was a miracle that I was not hurt, considering the way that I landed with the ball.

But the most important thing to me was when I saw the referee signal that the catch was good! The crowd was going nuts!

I did not realize the seriousness of this catch at the time. The only thing that mattered was that my team was in a position to score. I was thinking in my mind, "Come on, Eli, you've kept it together all this time; we need one more play."

It was like Eli heard me and moved forward with the plan. He threw another ball. This time it was in the direction of Plaxico Burress.

Fifty-nine seconds and counting. There was no time for a mistake. This was it! The pass Eli threw to Plaxico and his catch could not have been better executed. The ball floated in the air over Plaxico's head and dropped into his hands—and I lost control of myself. I fell to my knees and began to worship and thank God. My teammates were running on the field, yelling at the top of their voices, "We did it! We did it!" The extra point was good. Game over. Score: Giants 17, Patriots 14!

I could not help but hold my head down to my chest and say, "God, You did it!" I looked into the television set and gave a shout out to my mother in heaven. Then it was time to celebrate the miracle: We had finished our course on the road to victory. The curse of "almost and not enough" was broken. We did not die hard, and I know that what happened was only because of the intervention of God. I took great joy in saying, "God did it, God did it, God did it!"

—⁓—

As confused Patriot fans huddled together in a daze, hordes of Giants fans charged down from the stands to take over the field. Coach Coughlin got a cooler filled with ice and Gatorade dumped on his head.

My family members also ran onto the field as we moved toward the middle for the presentation of the Super Bowl trophy. Eli Manning was named the Most Valuable Player of the game. Within minutes of the buzzer, reporters dubbed the way I caught the ball against my helmet as "The Catch" and pronounced it to be the best play in Super Bowl history. These were honorable acknowledgements, but I know that every player on the team and on the sideline felt like MVPs and record breakers that night.

The next day the *New York Times* called "The Catch" "among the greatest plays in Super Bowl history."[1] Soon after that. *USA Today* agreed.[2] Ben Walker of the AP News Service called it the "Circus Catch."[3] Even Eli's brother, Peyton Manning, MVP of Super Bowl XLI, got in a comment: "Eli's pass to Tyree, I think, was one of the greatest plays of all time."[4] In an interview on June 1, 2008, with the Boston Globe, Rodney Harrison said, "I think you have to understand that certain things happen that you just can't explain."[5] Steve Sabol, president of NFL Films, said the catch had everything—drama, mystique, and even romance.[6] He said it was like a movie in itself—and I guess fans posting videos on YouTube must agree. If you look up this year's Super Bowl there, you'll find many different videos of those last ninety seconds.

What did I think when I saw that board lit up with the Giants' winning score? At first I was just in awe of what God had done and the way He had come through. I cried for a quick moment. I went through a bagful of emotions, but I had to go through them in about thirty seconds. That's all the time I had before the circus of postgame interviews began.

By the time I finished all the interviews and got back to the hotel, the first floor was one big party. Family and friends were welcome, and several of us celebrated the Lord. I finally got to talk a minute with Eli. He gave me a hug, and I thanked him for giving me the chance to make the plays. I'll never forget the way he slung that ball to me.

I slept well that night. I didn't get to bed until 2:00 or 3:00 a.m.! But I am not the kind to question God's working. It's not hard for me to believe. I didn't wrestle with it. I just rested in it.

COACH ALEEM, MONTCLAIR, NEW JERSEY

In the process of writing this book, my spiritual mom talked with Coach Aleem, my coach when I played in the Montclair Cobra Football League. The coach told Kimberly, "I was so proud of David at the Super Bowl game. I could feel electricity during that game. It was one of the greatest experiences of my life. It was also a great feeling to know that my labor was not in vain in my community. For some reason I dreamed about the big play that David made on January 29, six days before Super Bowl Sunday. I dreamed that Dave made the play of his life at the Super Bowl game. When Dave came down with the ball in the play with Eli Manning, I saw the dream unfold before my eyes. My hair literally stood up on my neck, and I was messed up for three days after the game. The miracle to me was that I saw the play in a dream before the game ever started. I have never experienced anything like it before in my life. I know that Dave is very spiritual. If someone would ask me about the play I would have to say, 'Yes, Dave's play was a blessing from God.'"

WHAT A PLATFORM!

The biggest thing about what happened on that field in Glendale is the platform God has given me to be a positive role model. As I told Derrin Horton in an ESPN interview after the game, we *are* role models. We have to step up to the board. It's not what we've asked for—it's what we've been given.[7]

NFL statistics show that Super Bowl XLII was the most watched Super Bowl in the history of the sport. Few can deny that something supernatural happened at Super Bowl XLII. It was more than a Super Bowl—it was a Supernatural Bowl! I have a double blessing—not only did I get to participate in it, but now I get to tell everyone about it. I've gone from the Giants player no one recognized to a guy who can't have a quiet, anonymous dinner at a restaurant anymore. That's a good thing, if I can share what God has done through me.

Jesus promises us more than once that the last will be first (Matt. 19:30; Luke 13:30). That promise came alive in my heart. As I looked back over the season, I noted that our last three victories were over teams that had beaten us all year. The Dallas, Green Bay, and New England games that we won to get the championship title were all upsets.

Here's the way I like to express what happened: The year 2008 is a year of **New** beginnings. When the **New** England Patriots faced the **New** York Giants...God did a **New** thing!

Not having Mom with me in Glendale to see her son win a Super Bowl ring was the only sadness I felt during that week, but I believe that one day we will sit down together in heaven and talk about the supernatural things that God did at Super Bowl XLII. There is so much that I do not understand about life and death. I have so many questions that only God can answer.

One thing I am confident about is that I will never question His will. The comfort that I have lies in the words from Romans 8:28: "And we know that all things work together for good to those who love God, to those who are the called according to His purpose." Though losing Mom so suddenly still did not make sense in my mind, my heart was at peace with the fact that God was working all things out for the good of my family. I believe that He really knows what is best for me, and in my worst moments He is still Lord! He has worked everything out for my good, and He will continue to do so.

Twelve

THE HALL OF FAITH

AN HONOR THAT LASTS FOREVER

Being noted in the Football Hall of Fame is one of the greatest honors an athlete can receive. There is a greater one, though. To be counted in the roll call of faithful men and women whom Paul lists in Hebrews 11 is an honor that will last forever. I have dedicated this chapter to Christian athletes who have excelled in the NFL and do not mind giving God the glory. It is important to me that I honor my brothers of the faith.

Many professional athletes have fallen prey to the temptations that come along with playing the game. This chapter testifies that there are men of God in the league who have stood firm on the profession of their faith. Their testimonies reinforce my testimony. Proverbs 27:17 says that iron sharpens iron, and I am honored to be a part of the "gridiron" of the Lord. I have played in the NFL with the Lord and without the Lord. Playing football with the Lord is so much better! A contractual agreement with a professional team means nothing if you are not on God's winning team. Words take on life and saving grace out of the mouth of as few as two or three witnesses. I pray that the testimonies of the witnesses in this chapter will stir your heart concerning what God is doing in the NFL.

DOORWAY TO THE HALL OF FAITH

TROY VINSON, PAST PRESIDENT, NFL PLAYERS ASSOCIATION

I know David Tyree as a great special teams player. His performance in the Super Bowl was unbelievable. God can step into any situation and use whomever He pleases. I am amazed how sometimes He chooses to use the person least expected and gets the job done. In those last few minutes of the game, God seemed to say to David Tyree, "I can use you because you will give Me the glory!" The catch that David Tyree made got the job done, and God surely got the glory! This is what playing in the NFL has been about in my life—accomplishing great things and remembering who to give the credit to.

I was blessed to retire from the NFL after fifteen great years. For fourteen of those fifteen years I have been married to my beautiful wife, Tommi. We have served God and raised our children in the admonition of the Lord throughout my entire football career. I have been awarded every humanitarian award that a player can receive in the NFL. But more important than every one of them is the opportunity I have had to serve my brothers in the NFL. As of March 2008, I am no longer president of the NFL Players Association. It has been an honor representing my fellow players and my Lord and Savior Jesus Christ. After five Pro Bowl games, four championship games, and nineteen play-off appearances, I can say that I retire from the NFL fulfilled. Playing the game and serving the men has been a blessing.

As I reflect on my career, I thank God for allowing me to be the seventh pick out of the first-round draft my senior year at the

University of Wisconsin. Statistics prove that the odds are against every young man in high school who has a dream of becoming an NFL player. More than one million high school seniors play football. Seventy thousand of those players will go on to play college ball. Out of seventy thousand players, nine thousand will be scouted, and approximately two hundred eighty will be drafted into the NFL. Finally, only one hundred twenty players out of the original one million high school seniors will play in the league for more than three years. Narrowing the numbers down even more, few players get to stand before the president of the United States and be presented with a Super Bowl championship ring. Think on these statistics as you read the testimonies in this chapter, and you will see that every player in it has received a miracle from God.

If you have aspirations to play in the NFL or in any other professional sport, remember that when God has something for you…it is for *you*! Do not be afraid to share your faith in your professional career. Some of the greatest players to play the game were God-filled. Reggie White, Cris Carter, Aeneas Williams, and Hardy Nickerson are a few. Charlie Ward was the greatest college football player to play the game. His road in life never led him to play NFL ball, but he did have a successful NBA career. Charlie was bold about his faith in God and was known to be sold out to the Father.

Nothing we pursue in life is achieved without the Maker of life. If you have not accepted Jesus Christ into your heart, receive Him today. If you are a believer, continue to put God first! Please do not look at me or the other guys who are doing great things in professional athletics. Keep your eyes on Jesus!

THE ROAD TO THE HALL OF FAITH

RENALDO WYNN, NEW YORK GIANTS, DEFENSIVE LINEMAN

- College: Notre Dame
- Notre Dame MVP; defensive lineman of the year; second team all-American; first-round draft pick (21st pick); twelve-year NFL veteran

I was honored when Pastor Kimberly Daniels asked me to work with her on the Hall of Faith project. Pastors Ardell and Kimberly Daniels were my pastors when I played for the Jacksonville Jaguars. I reconnected with them after seeing the Super Bowl game this year. I knew that their son, Mike, was on the team.

At the time of connecting with the Daniels, I was a free agent and unsure about my future in the NFL. I asked Pastors Ardell and Kimberly to pray with my family. We prayed in agreement for four months. To my surprise, I got a call from no other team than the New York Giants. What is the chance of that happening? On the day I received the call, my seven-year-old daughter was running around the room saying, "Call Pastor Kim, call Pastor Kim!" We asked her why, and she said, "We are going to the New York Giants, and my daddy will get a Super Bowl ring." I do not know if my daughter is prophesying or not, but it sure sounds good. The Bible says that out of the mouth of babes, God brings forth perfect praise. The thing that excites me is that she is paying attention to the things of God and believes that God can do it. I am looking forward to seeing what God does in the upcoming season. The overflow of David's testimony has already blessed me abundantly.

The day after Pastor Kimberly asked me to select the players, God gave me a dream. In the dream, He showed me the players I needed to ask to give their testimonies.

I am blessed to give my testimony in the Hall of Faith. I have been in the NFL for twelve years, and I give God the glory for every year. Coming into the NFL as a first-round draft pick has been a blessing to my career. I am sure that most of the players will agree that is probably the best situation to have coming out of college.

Like many other guys, I found out that the pressure of being a star football player in college can be challenging. I got a taste of the fast lane in college life and almost lost my mind. Up to my years in college I had never attended church. I did not have a conception of who God was. During that time in my life, if someone looked up the word *heathen* in the dictionary, *Renaldo Wynn* would have been next to it. Everyone admits that I was a real nice guy. From what I know now, I can testify that I was a nice guy on my way to hell.

My dream of being in the NFL almost became a nightmare when I was on the brink of losing my college scholarship. One day I was asked to attend an academic advisory meeting with twenty other scholarship athletes. The academic advisor got straight to the point. Without any apparent emotion he said, "You are the athletes that we do not expect to return next year!"

These words made my heart feel like it had dropped to the pit of my stomach. I was actually about to be kicked out of Notre Dame. The thoughts plagued my mind: What was I going to do? What would I go back to?

I did not have any other alternatives in life. A football scholarship was the only avenue I had to a prosperous destiny. My mother and father had no idea that I was flunking my classes. My mother was a schoolteacher, and my father was an alcoholic. My family was what would have been considered dysfunctional. My acceptance to Notre Dame was one of the greatest accomplishments in my family's history. My attending the college alone was a miracle. I went via the Southside of Chicago and had a full scholarship. This was unheard of.

As I listened to the words of the academic advisor, my dream seemed to vanish before my eyes. One of my coaches pulled me off to the side and said, "It will take an act of God for you to be eligible to play football again!"

Little did he know that God was about to act on my behalf. I did not know God, but somehow He surely knew me! Jeremiah 1:5 says God knew Jeremiah before he was formed in his mother's womb. My situation caused me to consider God. When I had never given Him the time of day, all of a sudden God was on my mind. One day I got down on my knees and asked Him for two specific things. I asked Him to help me to stay in school and to give me a wife. I promised God that if He would do these things, I would give my life to Him.

It would be real spiritual for me to tell you that I got up from prayer and went to the library and got enrolled in tutorial sessions. This was far from the case. Instead, I got in the car with a bunch of my buddies and headed for New Orleans to Mardi Gras. Even my friends thought I was crazy. They kept asking me, "How could you miss classes at a time like this?" Actions like this were common for me at the time, so it did not seem strange. I just wanted to live and let live!

When I did not know how to look out for myself, God in His infinite mercy saw fit to look out for me. What could have been a disaster became a huge blessing. In the midst of one of the biggest parties in the world, I met the love of my life. Tonya was walking around in all the festivities at Mardi Gras, and I knew that she would be my wife the first time I laid eyes on her. She played hard to get, but two months later, she was my wife.

Everyone really thought I was crazy for real by now. To get married in college was not a popular thing. My parents definitely thought it was a bad decision. The fact that I was about to be kicked out of college did not make things better.

Tonya moved into my apartment on campus right away. She set a new temperature in the house when she came. Tonya was a very ambitious young lady, and she had goals to do great things in life. It was also a blessing that she was a woman who did not mind pushing her man. One day I was lying in bed on the verge of skipping another class. Tonya turned over next to me and said, "I did not marry a failure. You had better get out of this bed and go to class so that you can make something out of yourself!"

Her words pierced my heart, and from that day forward I had a fresh incentive to do well in school. With a good woman by my side I was able to stay in college. Not only did I stay eligible to play football, but I actually became an honor-roll student also. My teammates and coaches could not believe the turnaround that I made. I experienced the real hand of God! I became a leader and a model player on the team.

Tonya and I started attending church, and in April 1997 we both gave our lives to the Lord. We have been serving Him faithfully since that time. I was drafted into the NFL immediately after I gave my life to the Lord. I have never had any regrets! We have a daughter, and I have enjoyed my family life as an NFL player. Every now and then a teammate will try to taunt me in front of the other players, saying, "Yeah, we are going to party tonight, but Renaldo's wife doesn't play that. The family boy has to go home!"

I just smile and tell them to enjoy themselves. My joy is living my dream playing football and having a wonderful family to share it with. There has not been one day in my career that I have missed the life I used to live. My family has been my strength in my career, and my wife and I have started an outreach ministry because of it. The name of our ministry is Family of Faith. We partnered with different organizations to bless children and their families during the holidays. God has given me so much joy as a husband and father, it is the least that I can do to share it with my community.

I have also enjoyed serving the players on my team as a player representative. There are so many players with the attitude of the old Renaldo. I believe that the Lord has called me to reach out to them. If God took me off of a crooked path and made it straight, He can do it for someone else.

I have known David Tyree as a player, but since the Super Bowl I have learned that he is a strong believer. As I sat watching the game with my family in my living room, I knew that something supernatural was going on. I could not put my finger on it. If someone told me that the game would have ended like it did, I would not have believed it. No one had to tell me... I saw it with my own eyes!

Oh, yeah, about *The Play*! First of all, David Tyree is a good player, but he operates behind the scenes. Rodney, his defender during the play, is the best in his field! When you think of the safety position in the NFL, anyone would say that Rodney is the man. Putting it the best way that I can, "David Tyree broke Rodney's heart in that play!" Players dread facing Rodney, and they think about him weeks before they have to face him on the field. It is no secret that Rodney is the most aggressive safety in the NFL. He stops a play by any means necessary! Yeah, at the Super Bowl, David broke his heart!

God seemed to orchestrate every little detail of that play. He had to anoint David to jump as high as he did. It is not a secret that David does not have the best vertical jump. The miracle started with the quarterback. The way he shook those defenders was an absolute miracle. As I look at the play over and over again, it is still unbelievable. I am a believer and it is unbelievable! The greatest part of the whole thing was to see how David gave God the glory. There is no doubt in my mind—not only was this game the best Super Bowl game I have ever watched, but the play was simply...supernatural!

MICHAEL JENNINGS, NEW YORK GIANTS, WIDE RECEIVER

- College: Florida State University
- Florida state high school champion quarter-miler finalist; Florida State track team (never played college football); third fastest 400-meter time at Florida State University; starting wide receiver in the World Bowl (NFL Europe); starting fifth year in the NFL

I am the poster child for getting into the NFL against all the odds. My mother is Apostle Kimberly Daniels, and she has written several books that tell the testimony of my road to the NFL. I had to evade a felony conviction to get into the NFL. My dream was to be an NFL player, but with a bunch of stupid mistakes, bad influences in my life, and a mad prosecuting attorney, my dream was about to be flushed down the toilet.

My mother was not a Christian when I was a young boy. Despite this, I should have made better choices in high school and college. I went through a lot in college because I made bad choices.

It was at the end of my senior year in college when I was faced with the felony charge. I was facing three to five years behind bars. I did not consider myself a bad person. I just wanted to have fun, and my fun did not line up with the laws of the land. I was not robbing people or breaking into houses. I was just hanging out with my boys, smoking a little weed, and joyriding on 24-inch rims.

What I considered joyriding the police considered reckless driving. I kept getting silly violations like having unauthorized tint on my windows, driving without a license, and tons of parking tickets. Every now and then I got caught with a blunt or two. Finally, I ended up before "the man" without much of a chance. The prosecuting attorney demanded three to five years with no other options.

I did not let my mother know what was going on until the last minute. My mom stepped in and did what she does best…she prayed! God knows that it paid off. I did do time in the local county jail, but God gave me a "Holy Ghost sentence." The words sounded sweet to my ears as the judge told my mother, "He will do sixty days in the county jail, but he can go to school and track practice in the daytime and report to jail at 6:00 p.m. every evening." I was allowed to maintain my civil rights and not be marked as a convicted felon for the rest of my life. More than that, I could still play NFL football.

This was all in the plan of God. When I was eight years old, a lady prophesied over me in church. She said that I would be an NFL player. Though it was my heart's desire, I had given up that dream. Traveling with my mom in the military did not give me a lot of opportunity to play football growing up.

I forgot my dream, but my mother never did. One day when I was in a lot of trouble, she sat me down and said, "Just as sure as I am a woman of God, if you will give your life to Jesus, the prophecy that was spoken over you to go into the NFL will come to pass!"

It sounded good at the time, and I did not have a lot of other options. When the prosecuting attorney said that I had to become a convicted felon because of all my prior cases, my mom never received it. She looked at me and said, "NFL players cannot be convicted felons, so he must be wrong. It does not line up with your destiny!" Thank God, she was right and he was wrong. I did those sixty days in jail, and they seemed like years. The food was atrocious. Because I left the jail every morning, I never had to eat there. I gave my food to guys who were really grateful to get it. I thanked God every day for being able to go on the outside to get a meal. Just looking at the slop they fed the inmates made me sick.

I also slept next to some inmates who seemed to be criminally insane. I was not a punk, but it was rough in the Leon County jail. My girlfriend dropped me off at 5:30 every evening, and I sat outside the jail praying with my mother each night before I checked in.

The feeling that I had every time I walked into that place was tormenting. I knew this was not my portion in life. God gave me a chance to choose. I asked myself over and over, "Do you want to be an athlete or a convict?" If I chose to live for the world, I had no choice but to be a convict.

I connected with my momma and chose God. Doors began to open for me to be the athlete that I had dreamed of being. I never got to play football at Florida State. With only two years of high school ball under my belt, I did not even know the rules of the game.

One day I ran the 40-yard dash at a meeting with some NFL scouts at Florida State. It was raining, and I had to run in bad weather with tennis shoes on. I clocked a 4.30 despite these obstacles. My time got the attention of some key people. I was promised a chance to go to Jerry Rice's training camp in California.

There was a little time before I went to the camp, and I had already graduated from college. I made a deal with my mother and moved home with her. I promised her that after I was released from jail, I would cut myself off from my friends and stay at home under her discretion. My friends and other family members were saying, "You're a man; you need to get out from under your momma." They did not understand that I was not just under her natural covering but her spiritual covering.

As a teenager, my mother went to Florida State on a track scholarship. She was an all-American sprinter and the fastest woman in the military for three years. She agreed to get me in shape for the NFL. She did not know the rules of football, so she bought me an NFL Madden video game to learn the rules. Every day for months I cleaned my mother's house for income and played the Madden game, by myself, all day long.

To make a long story short, I went to the Jerry Rice camp in such good shape that Jerry called the 49ers and the Raiders on my behalf. He told them how fast I was. I was in better shape than any of the other guys in the camp. My mom would always say, "Son, I don't know football, but there is nothing like a European track workout." I was signed by the San Francisco 49ers, and this began my road to the NFL. I was cut so many times that I really cannot remember the number. I will never forget the times I sat in a room waiting for a knock on the door. If no one knocked, that meant that I made it past the hatchet. A knock on the door meant, "Son, pack your bags. You're going home." I received so many knocks on my doors. When they came, I was back on my mother's sofa playing my NFL Madden video game again.

Eventually, the Lord supernaturally opened the door for me to go to NFL Europe. I also acquired a record of being cut in that league. I was told that I could not make the team because slots were already allocated to players who were sponsored by NFL teams. I heard the same thing every day: "Mike, you cannot make the team because you are not allocated."

My mother told me not to worry. She said, "Boy, you are allocated by Jesus!" I believed what she said so much that I had the words "Allocated by Jesus!" painted on the back window of my car.

Practices were bad because I never got a chance to show what I could do. One day they put me in, and I had a really good practice. Everyone was asking me to slow down. I was thinking, "I can't slow down; I've got too much against me." I ran like a bullet out of a gun. It was the day before the final cut, and I only had one chance. I had no choice but to make it good. I must have been impressive, because a man approached me after practice. He told me that I looked good. Then he said the words I had heard during the entire camp: "Son, you know that you cannot make this team because you are not allocated."

I thought to myself, "Tell me something that I don't already know!"

He then said something that got my attention for real: "When they cut you, I am going to sign you up for my team."

I was so happy that anyone wanted me on their team, and I started to rejoice! I settled down and turned back to the man to ask him what his name was and what team he coached. He slightly turned my way and said words I will never forget. "Son, my name is Bill Belichick, and I am the head coach for the New England Patriots."

I could not believe my ears! My momma's words had come to pass! I knew that God was real! The coach of the Super Bowl champions wanted me on his team. A team in NFL Europe did not have an allocation for me, but the Holy Ghost had a slot for me in the NFL. I eventually went to NFL Europe allocated, but I was in the door of the NFL. Coach Belichick gave me the opportunity to play the game for real. No more practice on video games! My first step to becoming a wide receiver was on the practice squad of the New England Patriots. I was eventually cut from the squad, but I was a better player. Coach Belichick promised that he would pick me up again.

I was temporarily signed by the Baltimore Ravens and then also released from their team. It seemed I would never make the roster of an NFL team. One night I had a dream that I was playing football in a New York Giants uniform. It was so real that I woke up and called my mother. I expressed how sad I felt when I realized that it was just a dream.

Though it was a dream, it was not *just* a dream—it was a dream that came true! The same day, only a few hours later, I was really called by the New York Giants!

I have been in the NFL for almost five years. Most of this time has been on practice squads. Last year I started for the first two games of the preseason and was unable to play for the rest of the season because of an injury. God has done so much that this slight detour did not distract me. I am in the NFL! I am on the other side of the Madden video game! My little brothers get a kick out of the fact that they can play me on the game. Dreams really do come true, and I believe in miracles!

I stood on the sideline in the University of Phoenix stadium on February 3, 2008, with no regrets. I was not going to let my injury discourage me—God had brought me too far. I was so happy to be in the NFL, and now I am the proud owner of a Super Bowl championship ring. I did not get to play, but thank God, I was on the team! Some of the greatest players in the league never received a ring. But I was on the team!

What did I think about the play that David Tyree made? The real miracle, to me, was that I was on the sideline when he made it. David is my close friend and a great player. The play was definitely another God thing! I have learned from my experiences in life that *nothing* is too impossible for God. He is not too busy to get involved with a football game, and He watches over us in everything we do in life. Wherever there is life...God is involved! I think that if we really paid attention to what was going on around us, we would see that miracles happen every day.

CORNELIUS GRIFFIN, WASHINGTON REDSKINS, DEFENSIVE TACKLE

- College: Troy State University/University of Alabama
- Eight-year NFL veteran

Getting into the NFL did not come easy for me, either. First of all, no one thought that I could get into college because of academic challenges. I came from a well-educated family, but I failed to apply myself in my studies. I attended Pearl River Community College and was noted as an all-American for two years. After sitting out for a year with no school or football, things looked really grim for me. After this, I went to Troy State University, where I began to apply myself academically. A cloud of doubt was over my head. All I could hear in my mind was, "You will never be eligible to attend a major university."

Despite this, the thought of my getting into a major university put a smile on my father's face. My father and mother were pastors, and they taught me to believe God. I was also taught that faith without works is dead. My father and mother were godly people, and they were examples at home. My father could care less about football, but getting an education meant the world to him. He himself was not educated and worked very hard. He always said, "I never want my children to work as hard as I had to work!" I watched my dad work from 6:00 a.m. on one morning to 1:00 or 2:00 a.m. the next morning. He never complained.

On June 8, 1998, a drunk driver tragically killed my father in a head-on collision. The devastation was more than I can describe. Being a family of faith, this loss was the last thing that we expected. In the midst of grieving the death of my father,

I was called to report to the football camp at the University of Alabama. It was a bittersweet moment because the loss of my father ruled my very being. I could not enjoy the good news under the dark cloud of loss. My mother would have to pastor our small church alone. My father's death really took a toll on her, and the transition was not easy. I was faced with making the decision to play football or to stay at home to support my family. As I looked into my mother's eyes, I knew the heart of my father. Her eyes said, "Go to school. This is what your father wanted!"

My first year of school was very challenging for me emotionally. I did not sleep a lot. I was wrapped in a knot with missing my father and thinking about what my family was going through at home. Playing football in the NFL was not my target in life. Getting an education was my goal. A football scholarship was the road to get me there. As a kid, I did have a dream of playing football in a major college, so this really fit in with my plan for an education. I never considered another option or even had a backup plan. Living the dream of going to a major university, I approached it by focusing on staying eligible and playing hard.

My father had taught me that if I focused on my education, God would honor my prayers and allow me to stay on scholarship. My quest to get a college degree prompted a dedication to football that caused me to excel on the field. As I was pressing toward an education, God gave me a career. Because of dedication to the game in college, I became the eleventh pick of the second round of the NFL draft. I was on my way to play for the New York Giants, and it was greater than I had ever dreamed! With twenty hours left to graduate, I signed an NFL contract and went to New York. Though I never finished my degree, I accomplished a successful career as an NFL player. One day I will complete my twenty hours of college and get my degree. Somehow I know that my father is in heaven smiling now.

My dad had more impact on my life than any other human being. Though I did not get a degree, I was spared the hard labor in life he had. I was given the opportunity to do something that I enjoyed doing and to make a career out of it. I do not believe that my father's desire for me was just about getting a degree. His vision for his children was about his desire for us to make something out of our lives so that we would not have to work under the curse of hard labor.

I work hard on the football field, but I enjoy every minute of it. My father raised seven children, and his mission in life was for us to have the best in life. I was the fifth child out of my seven brothers and sisters, and I am proud to be a product of my father's dream.

We did not have a lot in life, but what we had...we made count. My father always taught us to be good stewards. I believe that God blessed me to be in the NFL, and I had to be a good steward of that blessing. My testimony is not one of having a past of getting high and running after women. I was raised in the way of the Lord, and I did not depart. The trauma of losing my father as a young man had the positive effect of giving me the will to carry on my father's legacy. I know he is in heaven watching, and I simply could not do things that would not please him. I had no choice but to be the best that I could be. I had to do it to be an example to my brothers and sisters. I had to do it both for my heavenly Father and for my father in heaven.

It has not been a challenge for me to serve God in the NFL. I feel that it is easier to be saved than it is to sin. It is easier to serve God than to serve man. I always say, "I have only one Jesus to please, but there are so many people to please." I will retire from the NFL in a few years, and being a part of this Hall of Faith is a great accomplishment for me.

It is not so important that people remember how many sacks I got or how much money I made. I want to be remembered as a man of God. Many players thrive on being remembered by the "stats of the game." I also want to be remembered by my love for the game. My love for the game could only come from a changed heart through my Lord and Savior, Jesus Christ.

I thank God for my being a follower of Jesus in the NFL. It has made me a better husband, a better father, and a better teammate. I tell new players all the time, "Failure is not an option in God. Money with the wrong heart brings distractions, and finding peace with God secures peace within you."

What did I think of the Super Bowl? It blew my mind! David Tyree was highlighted in the game, and I was glad to find out that he is a faithful believer. When I knew David on the team in New York, he was not saved at the time.

It is awesome to see guys in the league turning their lives over to the Lord. I could really relate to David losing his mother two months before the game because of my experience with my father. David is known as a hard worker, and he is respected in the league as a special teams player. From my observation of the game, it is amazing that the "big play" went to David, with all the superstar players on the team. After all, he is "just a special teams guy."

I say this jokingly, as I believe God is looking for people who are "just who they are" so they can be highlighted for *who God is*!

If David had not made that catch, the Patriots would have made history, and the Giants would have gone back to New York the losers. David proved that he could hold his own. The defending safety, Rodney, had extremely tight coverage on him, and only God could have given David the power to hold on to that ball.

The play between David and Eli turned the game around. When I saw the play, I knew that the catch David made was for a reason and that New York would win the game. I have been watching football faithfully since the third grade, and I have never witnessed a play like that. It was a history-making play! It was an amazing game, and the catch was made so that God would be glorified.

DAVID PATTEN, NEW ORLEANS SAINTS, WIDE RECEIVER

- College: Western Carolina University
- Three-time Super Bowl champion; tied Walter Peyton's record; twelve-year veteran

My road to the NFL was definitely not a joyride. I was a free agent coming out of a 1AA school. I was raised in the church but backslid when I got to college. It was God's grace and mercy that I made it back in the church.

I did everything a young black man on a football team in college could do wrong. I did not get into the league from college, so I played Canadian and Arena League football. I worked hard before finally getting into the NFL.

I will never forget my hard labor in a coffee bean factory. I loaded four trucks with coffee bean bags on a daily basis. The bags weighed seventy-five pounds each, and I was working ten-hour shifts. I remember loading trucks and thinking, "That's it;

I give up on football. Lord, fill me with Your Spirit. All I want is to be saved!"

God humbled me to hear His voice during those hard days of labor. Football was my god, and the only true God taught me that there were more important things in life. My girlfriend at the time was also a great inspiration during my transition. She gave me an ultimatum. I remember her saying, "If you don't get yourself in place with the Lord, we can no longer have a relationship." I decided that she was the woman that I wanted to spend the rest of my life with, and I listened to her words.

While we were making plans to get married, USC held a Pro Timing Day. NFL scouts came in from everywhere. I was out of shape and had not worked out for four to five months. All I had been doing was lifting coffee bean bags. I prayed a simple prayer to the Lord: "Father, if it is meant for me to play, help me with this workout." Unfortunately, I was given the wrong time, and I walked into the tryouts late. This was not a good impression, and I already had enough stacked up against me.

I asked God to help me to run a 40 with the time of 4.5. The kid before me ran a 4.21. This did not make me feel good at all. I got down on the line, and by the time I had finished my race, I heard the timer say, "4.27." Without training, with no technique, and coming out of the coffee bean factory, I did it—or really, God did it! I ran the best 40 time of my life. I caught every ball and maximized my potential on every drill. I stood out in the midst of all the players who did drills, but this was apparently not good enough. Out of eighteen scouts, only one approached me. He spoke to me as if his mind was somewhere else, saying, "If things don't work for us in the draft, you are the kind of guy that I would look for."

I was thinking, "If you're not going to bring me to a tryout, I don't want to hear this." I went home with no hope of being looked at by a team.

The workout was on a Friday evening, and early Saturday morning my phone started ringing. I remember thinking, "Who could be calling me this early on a Saturday morning?"

As I put the phone to my ear, the voice on the line said, "This is the general manager of the New York Giants, and we want to bring you in for a tryout." My face lit up as I could hardly wait to get off the phone to pack my bags. I was immediately flown in to camp. I got dressed and prepared my mind to try out.

It seemed as though I was waiting in the locker room for a long time. Eventually, a man walked into the locker room and asked, "What are you doing here?" I told him that I was waiting to try out. He smiled at me and said, "You don't have to try out. Go in with the team to lift weights. We have already decided to sign you."

This was good news—but the road was still not easy. I went to camp as a "camp body." Somebody had to fill in slots so that the good players would not wear themselves out. Camp lasted for what seemed like forever, but it was really only two months. I gave it my all in all. I made it through three cuts and got released on the final cut.

The head coach came to me and said, "I did everything I could to keep you. We just did not have enough spots."

I had heard this story before, but this time I had just rededicated my life to the Lord. I was not moved because I figured that this was the will of God. I had only been married one week before camp, so I jumped into my car anxious to see my new bride. I drove thirteen hours home. It was not a sad trip because

I was excited about what God was about to do in my life. It was Jesus and me, and that was all that mattered. The god of NFL was dead in my heart.

When I got home, my wife greeted me with a puzzled look on her face. She said, "The Giants called and wanted to know why you left so fast. You were not supposed to leave."

I laughed and said to her, "What do they mean, why did I leave? They cut me!" It was true—they really wanted me on the roster of the New York Giants. I made the team! But God was so good that two other teams were calling for me at the same time. I had to choose between the Philadelphia Eagles, the Kansas City Chiefs, and the New York Giants. I chose the New York Giants because I had already learned their system and did not want to start over learning a new one. This was twelve years and three Super Bowl rings ago. I have been in the NFL since that time.

The road to the NFL was not an easy one for me, and that is why I reach out to guys like Michael Jennings. When he was being put on and off the practice squad with the New England Patriots, I allowed him to live with me. I knew what it was like trying to make it in the league. I wanted to plant a seed back into someone else because of what God has done for me. I brought him into my environment and purposed to live holy before him. He needed to know that players can live for Jesus in the NFL. I encourage all the young blood coming into the NFL that it takes maximum effort, good work ethics, and faith in Christ. My motto in life is this: "Never quit, and you will receive what is yours because what God has for you…is *for you!*" I also tell brothers that there are two things you can never do. You can never fool God, and you can never fool yourself. Be true to yourself, and you will succeed.

My favorite scripture is Psalm 37:4: "Delight yourself also in the LORD, and He shall give you the desires of your heart."

Yeah, I know David Tyree as a stable player! He is the "guru" of special teams. I experienced an emotional roller coaster watching the Super Bowl game. I have won three rings with the Patriots, but the Giants gave me my big break. One minute I was yelling for the Patriots, and then it would seem like the Giants had something going on behind the scenes that was working for them. When the Patriots scored with two minutes left in the game, I just knew it was over. I said to my family, "It's a wrap! Brady is at his best in last-minute games. There is no way these boys will drive against the Patriots' defense." I also said, "Eli has been up and down all season long. Surely, he cannot perform now!"

Then everything I thought and said was put to shame. Eli scrambled out from the hands of a slew of hungry defensive linemen and chunked the ball into the center of the field. The television camera was on Eli, so I had no idea who he was throwing it to. I assumed it was Toomer or maybe Smith. Surely it could have been Plaxico Burress. When the camera caught up with the ball, it was the last person that I expected it to be...David Tyree! With Rodney Harrison draped on his back, he held the ball to his helmet with one hand and landed on his back.

Who could doubt that this was the Lord? If anyone does, they just do not want to admit the truth. And to top it all off, I found out that David is a man of great faith. Oh, that is what's going on! God puts His people in places where the odds are against them so that He can get the credit. All He wants is the credit, and David sho 'nuff gave it to Him! The play between Eli Manning and David Tyree makes me say..."Surely that was nobody but the Lord!"

ANTWAAN RANDLE EL, WASHINGTON REDSKINS, WIDE RECEIVER

- College: Indiana University
- Super Bowl XL championship (first receiver to throw a touchdown in the Super Bowl); seven-year NFL veteran

As I pursued my NFL career, I was always told I was too short. I thank God for my mother. She looked into my eyes and said, "Do not pay those words any attention. God will bless you!"

God has always been with me to do what was required of me and more since the beginning of my NFL career. I was expected to run a 40 time of 4.5 or 4.6 at the combine that I attended coming out of college. The Lord touched my legs to run 4.42. Those were great days for a quarterback, which was the position I had played all of my life. The excitement of the draft drew near, and I was drafted as a second-round pick. I was single and had just given my life to the Lord as a senior in college. I adopted the philosophy of "faith, family, and then football." I knew that I had to get my life together before I went into the pros. It was no secret about the lifestyle of many professional football players. Conversations about the women, the gambling, and the drinking filled the college locker rooms.

As much as I loved being a quarterback, I was forced to become a wide receiver coming into the NFL. God knew what He was doing all the time, because I became one of the best wide receivers in the NFL. It really is true…God knows what is best for us.

I also prayed for the will of God in finding a wife. I needed His guidance because I only wanted to marry one time. God was faithful to send me a wife who loved the Lord. Coming into the NFL, I knew that I had to keep my head on straight. When you are a star athlete, so many people tend to tell you how great you are. I made sure that I surrounded myself with people who loved me enough to tell me the truth. I also found strength in studying the Word of God and living by it. I did not want to serve God as a hypocrite; I wanted to give Him my all. I felt that the most important thing in my life was to put God first. I had such a hunger to know His will for my family and me.

My mother has been saved since I was a young boy, and all I can remember is going to church. When my father got saved, our house went bananas over Jesus. We started attending church even more than before. I realize that God is the keeper of a man's soul, but my mother and father's spiritual influence was a strong force in my life. I did not understand when I was younger, but the importance of being in church became a revelation to me as I got out on my own. I treasured this foundation and wanted it for my wife and children.

My testimony is that I was raised in the way of the Lord. I do not have a lot of "football with the devil" stories. I do not judge the guys who do, but it just was not my portion. I left home and learned to seek God for myself. The devil would have stolen everything I learned in church if I allowed him to.

I have made some mistakes in life, but I have no regrets. If I could change anything in my life, I would have waited and not had sex before marriage. But even after fornication...God still delivers! Today I have a strong marriage, and we have experienced miracles from God in my house.

Last year my wife gave birth to my youngest girl, Aunna. My wife, Jaune, had blood clots from her ankles to her heart after the delivery. The doctors gave up on my wife and said that there was nothing they could do. We knew what to do, and we turned to

God in prayer! We called everyone we knew to pray for my wife's healing. She stayed in the hospital for ten days as we endured all the negative reports. They said she would never have children again because she also had blot clots on her ovaries. As the negative words were released from the mouths of the experts, I had no choice but to depend on what I had learned in the Word of God. We took authority over the situation and did not allow anyone who was in doubt to be in my wife's room. We filled that room with the truth through prayer and praise. By God's mercy and His awesome power, my wife was miraculously healed. The doctors said that they had never witnessed anything like it before. Even as my wife was under attack, they could not believe that she was not in pain. We enjoyed the presence of the Lord as the symptoms had to submit to our faith in God.

Despite the lies of the devil, as I write this, my wife is pregnant again. I know that God is a miracle-working God. Whether He is moving in the hospital room or on the football field, He is still working miracles today!

Yes, I believe that the play between David Tyree and Eli Manning was an absolute miracle. The confirmation is that it was named "the greatest play in Super Bowl history." As I was watching the game, I saw Eli running from those linemen for his life. The supernatural catch that David made not only made me rub my eyes to see if it was real, but it also was made against the best safety in the league. The best team, with the best record, with the best quarterback and coach, was interrupted by a supernatural intervention that cannot be denied!

There is no question this game was monumental. There is no way that David could have held on to that ball by his own power and might. When I found out that he was sold out to the Lord, things began to make more sense. The only way that play could be explained is that God did it! It was a miracle before the eyes of the world and a blessing to a man of God who deserved it. Many do not think God would get involved in a football game. I say that He does. Where people are involved, God is involved.

It is not about the game but about the souls that can be won if the right man gets the right platform. David Tyree was the right man in Super Bowl XLII! I pray that athletes around the world will get a revelation that God wants to be involved in their everyday affairs. The Bible says that it does not prosper to win the whole world and lose your soul.

The other day I was listening to an interview with Tom Brady of the New England Patriots. He has won three Super Bowl championships, been named the NFL and Super Bowl MVP, and yet still confessed having a void in his life. Whenever there is a void, only Jesus can fill it! This is why I am bold in my faith.

So many players have voids in their lives. The notoriety of being an NFL player does not give you peace at night or joy in the morning. I cannot straddle the fence in my faith because I have to live a lifestyle that will let my brothers know that they have a choice. They do not have to turn to things in life that will only cause pain. I want them to admire the God in me and consider Jesus when the challenges of life get them down.

JAMES THRASH, WASHINGTON REDSKINS, WIDE RECEIVER

- College: Missouri Southern State College
- Played in three NFC championships; twelve-year NFL veteran

I went to college at a Division II school and did not get a lot of recruitment for the NFL. I entered the NFL as a free agent and signed my first contract with the Philadelphia Eagles. It was difficult to make a squad with my status. First of all, the guys who were drafted with bonuses had a head start on guys like me. I also had to compete with the players who were returning on the team.

With the odds against me, I was cut from the squad before the training camp began. Two days later I was picked up by the Washington Redskins. I got the break of a lifetime in the first two preseason games by running two kickoff returns all the way back. By the last cut I was still on the team and started wearing the Washington Redskins jersey.

During my rookie year I did not go to church. I eventually started attending church, but I was not dedicated to it at the time. I repeated the sinner's prayer, but my actions revealed I did not mean it in my heart. I was just doing that "religious thing" because there were parts of my life that I was not ready to give up.

I "played church" for three years until I had a supernatural encounter. I was in my town house lying down, listening to music, and I felt like I was being held down. I jumped up and ran around the house checking to see if someone was in my house. It was so real! As I stood with my heart beating fast, I heard a voice clearly say, "You've been living a lie. Choose life or death!"

Even if something tried to convince me that the voice was not real, I knew that the voice was telling the truth. Around believers, I was "amen, bless you," and with nonbelievers I would fit in just as well. I was not grounded in that solid rock that comes from truly surrendering to God and His Word. I was trying to fit in both at church and with my worldly friends. I had convinced myself that I could handle both, but God was letting me know that trying to love two worlds is hard to do.

This experience brought conviction to my heart, and I chose life! I did not join a church or just say words out of the side of my mouth. I had a real experience with God. I met the Father, but I think it would be better to say that He met me! Jesus met me right where I was. It was the real thing this time, and I knew that I had to lay anything down that would not please Him.

I had been married one year before my encounter with the Lord. My beautiful bride, Amber, was a church girl who grew up in the traditions of religion. I never told her about what happened to me in the house that day. Two months later she confronted me, saying, "For two months I have noticed a change in you." I knew that it was time to explain to her what I had experienced. Once I told her what had happened, we praised God together. We knew that the Lord had worked a miracle in my soul. What God had done in my life witnessed to my wife. Immediately, she got stirred up about the things of the Lord. She was no longer just a church girl! She caught fire to serve the Creator of the heavens and the earth.

The devil was not just going to lie back and let me serve the Lord without getting busy. I started receiving pressure from the guys on the team. They seemed to want me to be the same person that I was before I got saved. As I expressed the fact that there were certain things I did not do anymore, some of my teammates did not understand. This did not bother me so much because I knew that they would understand sooner or later. I was in it with God for the long haul.

I know David personally, and we often encourage each other when our teams play. I was proud of David when he made the

Pro Bowl, and I have watched him come a long way in his walk with God. The good thing is that he is sold out to the cause of the gospel. When Eli Manning threw the ball down the field, my heart rejoiced when I saw number 85 come down with it. I cannot help but be happy. It could not have happened to a better guy. David has always been a great player, but he performed when it counted the most. The opportunity came, and he took advantage of it. Yes, God used him!

Thirteen

THE CYCLE OF SUCCESS

This Book of the Law shall not depart out of your mouth, but
you shall meditate on it day and night, that you may observe
and do according to all that is written in it. For then you shall
make your way prosperous, and then you shall deal wisely and
have good success. Have not I commanded you? Be strong,
vigorous, and very courageous. Be not afraid, neither be
dismayed, for the Lord your God is with you wherever you go.

—JOSHUA 1:8–9, AMP

T here are different kinds of success. First, there is temporary success, which only lasts for a moment. Then there
is overnight success that seems to happen haphazardly
and just by chance. Joshua 1:8 mentions "good success." This is
the kind of success that is eternal. It is *God success*! I call it *the*
cycle of success because it is success that continues to flow because
God is the source.

Success is the achievement of goals that have been set to
accomplish assignments according to a plan. Success must have
a vision, or there is nothing to measure it by. I feel confident in
saying that vision is the beginning of success. Taking it further,

I must add that the foundation of a person's vision is rooted in their motive.

Let's talk about motives. The reason a person wants to achieve a goal is very important. Take a moment and visualize a goal that you have set in your life. Write down three reasons why you want to accomplish this goal.

1. _____

_____

2. _____

_____

3. _____

_____

Think about the goals you have visualized and ask yourself these questions:

- Are your goals selfish, or do they consider people who are close to you in your life?
- Do your goals have repercussions that will affect you in a negative way?
- Do the three goals you have listed conflict with each other?
- Do these goals conflict with things already established in your life that make you unwilling to sacrifice to accomplish your goals?

- To accomplish these goals, will you have to compromise your integrity?
- Are these goals really your heart's desire, or are you pursuing them for the sake of someone else?

This little evaluation is a checklist of things that will help you to make sure that your first step for success is secure. Motives are everything! God looks at the heart of a man or woman. In fact, God moves by motives! How many young boys have the dream of playing in the NFL or some other professional sport? I am sure that there are too many to count. That question leads to some others: Why do they want to be professional athletes? Is it because they have seen so many athletes riding around in nice cars with pretty women? Are they in competition with rivals to prove that they can make it? Do they want to play sports and bring their drug-dealing friends into the league to get other players strung out on dope?

These are extreme situations, but I use them to make a point: if the motive of a vision is not right, it will not lead to good success!

This is a lesson to be learned. All success is not good success. Good success is *God success*!

In the first chapter of Joshua, God taught Joshua how to get good success. Joshua was given motivation and warning on the topic of good success. God told Joshua:

1. Do not allow the *Word* of God to depart from your *mouth.*
2. *Meditate* on the *Word* of God day and night.
3. *Observe and do* all that is written in the Word.
4. You shall make your way *prosperous.*

5. You shall *deal wisely*.
6. You shall have *good success*.
7. Be *strong* and *courageous*.
8. Do *not fear* or be dismayed.
9. God will be with you *wherever* you go.

Joshua was a young man who was faithful to God, and he had a role model in Moses. As a young man I have found it beneficial to have role models in my life. Any great vision needs a plan. It also needs a pattern, a schematic of someone else's life you can use as a pattern for living your own life. Not only did Joshua watch Moses, but he also had his "DNA." Moses imparted the ability to succeed into Joshua's life. When Moses was gone, Joshua had a standard to live by, and Moses's spirit was on him. Joshua was serving God first, and his motives were right in following the path that Moses had laid out. This gave him what he needed to carry out the legacy of God for the next generation.

It is important that we evaluate our motives. This has nothing to do with being a good person or a bad person. On the road to success there are stumbling blocks that have no respect for who we are. These stumbling blocks can trip whoever is vulnerable. As a matter of fact, people whom others judge to be "good people" are more vulnerable to being tripped up on the road to success. The apostle Paul warns, "Therefore let him who thinks he stands take heed lest he fall" (1 Cor. 10:12).

Patterns for Success

The nine points from the Book of Joshua I've listed above can be jewels in our crown, or they can be rocks around our necks. I believe that the Lord gave them to us as patterns for success in every area of life. I encourage you to grab hold of them and treasure them. Words of wisdom produce life, and the life Jesus promises to those who follow Him always succeeds. There is no failure in God!

These words were meant to be a blessing to Joshua if he obeyed them. If he chose to ignore them, they would become a curse. Jesus said that unto whom much is given, much is required (Luke 12:48). This is an important principle to live by. After Joshua received instruction from the Lord, he was held accountable for what God had given him. Many young men do not succeed in life because they are not accountable to what they have been taught.

Have you been accountable to what you know? Can you take the principles listed above and apply them to your life and know that your motives for success are secure? Let me put the instructions into simple terms:

- Continue to confess the Word of God from your mouth.
- Do not speak negative confessions.
- Do not be double-minded.

It is imperative that your confessions become arrows to spearhead what you are pursuing in your life. So confess the Word of God and meditate on it.

THINK ON THESE THINGS AND THEN DO THEM

Meditating on the Word of God is important and powerful. Other forms of meditation that leave out the Word of God are only counterfeits of the real thing. God created meditation for His people. The Bible says that as a man thinks, *he is*! (See Proverbs 23:7.) In the natural, *you are what you eat*. Spiritually speaking, *you are what you think.* If you think negative thoughts, you will get negative results.

The apostle Paul was a successful man. He gave us instructions to meditate on things that are true, honest, just, pure, lovely, of a good report, virtuous, and full of praise (Phil. 4:8). These are the kinds of things that successful people think on. There is no room for failure in their minds.

I admire the Old Testament's King David because he was not a perfect man. Like me, another David, he had some indiscretions in his life, but he overcame them all. Before I came to know the Lord, I was an alcoholic. You have read in this book about my blackout episodes. Alcohol was my god! It dictated to me and ordered my steps. You have also read of the episodes of unprotected sex I engaged in and of the sexually transmitted disease I contracted. I remember waking up in bed and not knowing the person next to me. I could not possibly be faithful to Leilah because I was so unfaithful to myself. I would laugh it off with the guys on the team, but I was so ashamed. I was bound and wanted help, but I did not know where to start. When Leilah gave me an ultimatum, I looked into her eyes and I knew she meant it: "David, you have to choose me and your children or your lifestyle." I thank God that I made the right choice, the choice that leads to good success in ways that count for eternity.

Are you in bondage as you are reading this book? Maybe it's to women or alcohol or drugs, but it can be other things too, whatever rules your life instead of God. Whatever you are going through, you can give it to God today. It was not too late for David, and it's not too late for you!

Even after all David did, the Bible calls him "a man after God's own heart." This may blow the minds of religious people because

David was an adulterer and a murderer. What is my point? You do not have to be perfect to be successful! Some of the most successful people I know have been through hell. How did they come out of it? I can start by suggesting how you can come out of it. The first step is recognizing your faults and dealing with them. David did not hesitate to repent. Most of the time, he repented as he meditated before the Lord. Meditation is medicine when you put your mind on the right thing. The Book of Psalms confirms that David was a man of meditation.

These passages about the importance of meditating on God's Word have meant much to me. I pray that they will bless you:

> His delight is in the law of the LORD, and in His law he *meditates* day and night.
>
> —Psalm 1:2, emphasis added

> When I remember You upon my bed, I *meditate* on You during the night watches.
>
> —Psalm 63:6, emphasis added

> I will also *meditate* on all Your work, and talk of Your deeds.
>
> —Psalm 77:12, emphasis added

> I will *meditate* on Your precepts and contemplate Your ways.
>
> —Psalm 119:15, emphasis added

> Princes also sit and speak against me, but Your servant *meditates* on Your statutes.
>
> —Psalm 119:23, emphasis added

My hands also will I lift up to Your commandments,
which I love, and I will *meditate* on Your statutes.
—Psalm 119:48, emphasis added

Let the proud be ashamed, for they treated me wrongfully
with falsehood; but I will *meditate* on Your precepts.
—Psalm 119:78, emphasis added

My eyes are awake through the night watches, that I may
meditate on Your word.
—Psalm 119:148, emphasis added

Meditate on these things; give yourself entirely to them,
that your progress may be evident to all.
—1 Timothy 4:15, emphasis added

God also told Joshua to *observe and to do* what He commanded.
Laziness and procrastination are not ingredients in the formula
for success. To be successful in anything, you must be a *shaker*
and *mover*! Meditation helps you to be focused to get things
done.

The Nike company coined the phrase "Just Do It," but it has
been a biblical principle for a long time. *Nike* (pronounced *nee-kay*) is a Greek word for success or victory in the New Testament;
it is the symbol of a champion. Success is more than a professional word or a personal goal. It is a spiritual principle! You
cannot lie around and wait for success to fall down upon you. It
is reserved for those who will take by force what is already theirs.
God told Joshua, "You shall make your way prosperous." What
are *you* waiting for? Get up and bust a move!

VISION BRINGS PROVISION

Another important principle to remember is this: With vision there is *provision*. Though people may be placed in your path to support you along the way to your promise, you must draw from that God-given ability *inside you* to prosper.

Deuteronomy calls it the "power to get wealth" (Deut. 8:18). This wealth does not only refer to money or riches. It also refers to strength, valor, force, substance, and war-worthiness. To be "war-worthy" means that God put a drive inside you to fight for what is rightfully yours. Joshua had everything within himself that he needed to succeed. When God told him, "You shall make your way prosperous," He was saying that Joshua had to do something! The only way he could fail is if he did not do his part. A great fallacy in Christianity has been: "Just believe and you will receive." Just to sit on your hands and expect things to happen is not enough—the apostle James says, "Faith by itself, if it is not accompanied by action, is dead" (James 2:17, NIV).

DEAL WISELY

God also instructed Joshua to *deal wisely*. Wisdom is a foundational principle. Anytime you deal with foundations, there are lessons to be learned. Having knowledge without wisdom is like giving a three-year-old a pistol with bullets to shoot. That three-year-old has a powerful weapon in his or her hand but does not have the skill to operate it. Wisdom enhances our skills to operate in our gifts. Even gifts need skills to carry them out. This is why training is so important. I know a lot of young men who have great athletic gifting. But these young men will never succeed in a sport until they get with a coach to train them so that they can become skilled. What great athlete can be his or her own coach?

Let's look at what it means to be skilled:

- A skilled person is one who has developed proficiency through training.
- A skilled person is proficient as a result of experience.
- A skilled person has abilities he has gained through someone else's instruction and oversight.

It scares me how some professional athletes get the big head and resist the training and instruction of their coaches. A coach-player connection is important to achieve ultimate success in a sport. That connection happened on our team this year. Coach Coughlin and we players obtained a coach-player connection that demanded success. As Coach Coughlin submitted to the needs of his players and they yielded to his leadership, the rest is history.

Yes, he was the head of the team, but winning the trust of his players made the vision succeed. Just as God calls a husband-and-wife team to submit to each other, there needs to be a submission covenant between players and coaches. As Coach Coughlin found out, mutual submission makes a vision move forward.

BE STRONG IN GOD'S PROMISES

Finally, God told Joshua to *be strong and not fearful*. He promised him that He would be with him everywhere he went and give him good success. Good success is success that makes you feel good about yourself when you wake up in the morning and go to bed at night. Good success—*God success*—keeps the cycle of success flowing in your life.

Good success gets down in your heart. It never runs out!

Motive | Vision | Success | Incentives

Success has a flow, and when the flow begins, the result is inevitable. Whether you look at it biblically or professionally, there is a pattern for success. It doesn't happen overnight, and you cannot get out of it what you have not put into it.

Young men who turn to illegal activities like selling drugs only have a form of success that is seen from the outside. It is temporary and does not continue to flow. But good success gets down in your heart and makes you feel good about yourself. It never runs out!

This is the pattern God has given me for success:

MOTIVE	This is the root word for motivation. It means to be driven (pushed), impelled (launched), or incited (stirred up) to take action on something.
VISION	To have perception and intelligence that mentally produces foresight to get things done.
SUCCESS	To obtain something desired and planned; accomplishing set goals.
INCENTIVES	Rewards that incite motives.

When your motives are right, it gives power to your vision. When you grab the vision and walk it out, you will succeed. Success has incentives that reinforce your motives, and the cycle of success starts over and continues to flow. Remember: it never runs out!

GOD WANTS US TO SUCCEED

I am a blessed man. I have always done what was required of me as a student in school. I obtained an athletic scholarship from Syracuse University where I graduated with a bachelor's degree in consumer studies. I have a beautiful wife who loves the Lord and has given me four children. I went to the Pro Bowl during my rookie year in the NFL, and now I am a Super Bowl champion. God also allowed me to have a history-making catch under my belt. I consider these things successful, but I have not arrived and cannot stop there. Success is not a place you visit. It is a place that you build and live in to make your home.

Many people experience success and somehow lose it along the way. The first thing we need to understand is that God wants us to succeed. He promises that *whatever* we put our hands to the plow to do, we will prosper! He also said that *wherever* the soles of our feet should touch, the land would be ours. So how does God want us to succeed? With whatever and wherever! There are no limitations in God.

KEYS TO SUCCESSFUL ENDURANCE

- Stand for what you believe in despite all opposition.
- Do not allow yourself to fall into the bondage of what other people think.
- Commit to be open to what you are not familiar with.

- Do not be distracted if the path of success seems different from what you had imagined it to be.
- Never get stagnant or too comfortable where you are—there is always a next level.
- Never lose sight of your dream.
- Always take time to reflect on what is most important in your heart.
- Prepare yourself by setting goals and nurturing them along the way.
- Be ready when an opportunity arises.
- Never say "never," "I can't," or "I do not have."
- Watch out for wrong confessions—they are the enemies of your success.
- Be faithful over small things, and you will be promoted when the time comes.

I pray that these keys will bless you as they have blessed my family and me.

Fourteen

THE INGREDIENTS OF GREATNESS

Another parable He put forth to them, saying: "The kingdom of heaven is like a mustard seed, which a man took and sowed in his field, which indeed is the least of all the seeds; but when it is grown it is greater than the herbs and becomes a tree, so that the birds of the air come and nest in its branches."

—MATTHEW 13:31–32

A WORD WITH MANY MEANINGS

Greatness can be defined as:

- Large in size
- Remarkable in degree
- Outstanding in importance
- Superior in quality
- Powerful in nature
- Influential in contact
- Distinguished in the eyes of others
- Skillful in the use of one's hands

When I think of greatness, though, none of the above definitions comes to mind. Greatness means so much more to me.

- The power of greatness is having the ability to come from a place of small beginnings into a place of great increase.
- The essence of greatness is not who you are or where you are, but who you have become in comparison to who you used to be.
- Great people have roots that afford them an eternal source that never dries up.
- Greatness is deeper than overnight success or what other people can see.
- Greatness is something you have to hang around, soak in, and get a revelation of.
- One act does not determine greatness.
- Greatness has endurance and longevity that cannot be limited to what can be done in an instance.

I have met many well-accomplished people. Accomplishment does not necessarily make a person great. What is considered great in the eyes of men should be put next to the Word of God to see if it actually measures up to what God considers great. We must ask this question: By what standard do we measure greatness? Greatness in the eyes of one man can be failure in the eyes of another.

I feel it is very important for you to understand how I view greatness. Let it be known to all that greatness cannot be limited to a catch at the Super Bowl! Yes, it was an awesome catch and a great moment, but great moments do not determine great men. How men *handle* moments like these determine their greatness.

Ephesians 1:18–19 speaks on what greatness is all about. It talks about how the eyes of our understanding need to be enlightened to know the hope of our calling. It also mentions the exceeding greatness of God's power to believers. This power is rooted in Christ, fulfilled when God raised Him from the dead and set Him at His right hand in heaven.

Matthew 13:31 teaches that the kingdom of heaven is like a grain of mustard seed, which is so small it is almost impossible to see—the least of all seeds. When this seed is fully grown, it becomes the greatest of all the herbs. It grows up to become a tree with large branches. These branches grow to become so strong that birds can sit on them and be fully supported.

THE INGREDIENTS OF GREATNESS

These verses from Ephesians and Matthew reveal the ingredients of greatness.

1. EVERY HUMAN BEING HAS THE POTENTIAL INSIDE TO BE GREAT.

This potential is the *seed of greatness* symbolized by the mustard seed in Matthew 13. God created every human being with the ability to do great things. The challenge that many people have is being able to identify that greatness deep within. Once they do identify it, they must nurture it so that it can grow into maturity. Growth is the root power of greatness, because without it even big things can seem nominal. If anything ceases to grow, life is cut off. Without life, nothing can be great.

Jesus came into the world that we might have life and have it "more abundantly" (John 10:10). Many people attempt to have an abundant life without having a revelation of what the essence of life is. Having a revelation of the essence, or root, of life is a key to opening the doors of true greatness.

A medical missionary working in the bush of Africa is just as great as the most accomplished televangelist in the world. The greatness of each person can be measured only by the potential inside. This measurement is based on whether or not we do what is in us to do.

You cannot put an orange next to a grapefruit and measure sweetness. The seed of the grapefruit does not have the same characteristics inside it as the seed of the orange. God created them to be different from each other and to serve separate purposes. Just so, God has placed the unique seed (potential) of greatness in each person so that each of us can do what God specifically created each of us to do. An important ingredient of greatness is knowing who you are and what you are called to do.

2. GREATNESS IS THE ABILITY TO KNOW THE HOPE OF YOUR CALLING AND HAVE COMPLETE FAITH IN GOD.

Most college students change their majors many times before they settle down in a career. It is a curse to be a "jack of all trades and a master of none." Greatness has the ability to target and master. As a young boy I identified with becoming a football player to get a college scholarship. Because of the seed of greatness on the inside of me, I attained goals much greater than I could have imagined. When you are faithful over little things, God will give you the ability to rule over much.

An ingredient of greatness is *the ability to be focused*. Distractions will hinder faithfulness because it draws you into too many directions. You cannot be faithful where there is no focus. When I was in middle school I played several sports. As I matured in my calling to play football, I targeted my focus in that direction.

3. GREATNESS IS ATTAINED WHEN YOUR POWER IS ROOTED IN SOMEONE GREATER THAN YOURSELF.

The Ephesians 1 passage above describes the greatness of God's power to believers. Many professional counselors suggest that their clients should depend on "a higher power." To an extent I agree, but I am biased as to who is worthy to be that higher power they depend on. For a believer, the power on which we depend is Christ—greatness is having faith in Christ! We believe that He is Lord of lords. We do not deny that there are other gods. We do deny that they are on the same level as Jesus. He is God all by Himself!

I believe that Jesus Christ is not just a higher power, but *the Highest Power*! He is Lord of lords and King of kings. I feel sorry for atheists and agnostics who either insist that there is no God or debate whether He exists. There are many public figures who are considered great in the eyes of men. When they try to define God using secular mind-sets or spiritualism or intellectual arguments, they fail. They stand before multitudes and pretend to have the answers to life's questions and lead millions astray. The truth is that these people have no hope! Where Jesus is not Lord, there will be no hope. There will always be something missing without His presence on the throne of a person's heart. It is simple: no Jesus; no hope!

A person who does not have hope is doomed to be subject to all the miseries of life. The only hope is to know that God exists. Without faith in His existence, there are no answers to life's problems.

Great men know their God and carry out great exploits in His strength! They are not afraid to depend on God. I am so glad that I am not the final authority in my life. My authority is limited, but God is omniscient (He knows all), omnipresent (He is every-where), and omnipotent (He has all power).

4. GREATNESS IS UNDERSTANDING THAT THE WAY UP IS DOWN AND HUMILITY IS THE KEY.

The power of the ministry of Jesus Christ when He walked the earth was humility. As powerful as Jesus was, He was a servant. Great men understand that any good leader must be a servant first. People who have never served make terrible leaders and cannot tap into true greatness. The greatest act of humility ever recorded was when God Himself died on the cross for our sins. He stepped down from glory and allowed to happen to Him what should have rightfully happened to us. We were guilty, but He bore our sicknesses and infirmity. Who could not serve a God like this?

Jesus could have called down thousands of angels to destroy His persecutors, but He did not. The essence of humility is when a person humbles himself or herself when he or she really did not have to do so. God came down from heaven and walked in the flesh. He was spit upon, beaten, and persecuted. Before He ever ascended to heaven, He even descended to hell. Imagine the horror of that visit—and yet He did it willingly.

Great men do not press their way to get to the front of the line. They understand that because there is a seed of greatness inside them, promotion is inevitable when the time comes. Real greatness cannot be denied. It makes room and opens doors that always give God the glory. Great men never take the credit! They humble themselves under the mighty hand of God and give Him the glory.

5. GREATNESS DOES NOT DESPISE SMALL BEGINNINGS.

Small beginnings are great! This can only be seen by focusing on *quality*, not *quantity*. Since I became a Christian on March 14, 2004, my perspective on life has changed dramatically. I have learned that the way I perceive things affects how I deal with them. Small beginnings are gifts from God, and all greatness must start there. Overnight success has taken many people out. We must grow with greatness to be able to handle increase in our lives. As we witness on television and in magazines daily, not everyone can handle increase.

Great men understand that they are born with the potential for greatness inside them. They know that they will lose this potential if they are not willing to endure the process. This process entails allowing God to take them from one level of glory to the next. Too much glory from the world all at once has stifled the potential of many great men and women. I have learned to be content with my portion and wait on God. At the same time, I understand how to move forward when I step into my season.

6. GREATNESS COMES THROUGH GROWTH AND THROUGH REACHING A MATURITY THAT CAUSES A PERSON TO HOLD UP WHAT ONCE HELD THEM DOWN.

Think again of that mustard seed. It is the smallest of herbs, but God created it to grow up to become a great tree with large branches.

Many small seeds are eaten by birds before they have a chance to grow. This was not the case in the Bible's story about the mustard seed. Instead, this seed became a tree with branches large enough for birds to sit upon. The powerful truth of this parable is this: *As we grow to maturity, the things that used to hold us down will become things we can hold up!*

Let me give an example: I used to have an addiction to alcohol. I do not believe that I am a "recovering" alcoholic. I am *delivered* from the thoughts, taste, and desire to get drunk. I am not recovering; I am totally free! When Jesus made me free, there were no more struggles.

The birds in the parable represent the alcohol addiction that could have devoured me. I have grown up and out of that situation, and now my branches are strong. This means that I am strong enough to help others who may be struggling with this bird of addiction (alcoholism). They can sit on my branches now! This is what greatness is about—walking in the power of it so we can help another person in need.

MY HALL OF GREATNESS

Everyone has certain people whom they admire. These four people deserve a place of honor in my personal *Hall of Greatness*.

REGGIE WHITE (MY PEER)

We all need to have peers in our lives whom we look up to and consider great. It is important to give honor to people to whom we can relate. It is a terrible thing to become so familiar with a person that you cannot acknowledge greatness in that person's life. Reggie White was a great NFL player, husband, father, and believer. For years I have admired the way he handled himself on and off the field. He was a great spiritual leader in the league and caused many souls to come to Christ. His witness made him great. Reggie had the ability to impact everyone he came into contact with, and he knew how to affect his environment for Jesus. God bless his soul.

BISHOP CHARLES HARRIS (MY SPIRITUAL FATHER)

Bishop Harris is my pastor and spiritual father. He has covered my family and me since I gave my life to Jesus. I honor him as a spiritual leader in my life. I call him a great man because I have watched him walk in integrity and be an example to men in the kingdom of God. He has been consistent in his faith walk, and his integrity is unquestionable. He teaches sound doctrine from an uncompromising position and has provided a safe haven for my family and me to worship. He has raised me up in the things of God and helped me to have a strong foundation in Christ. He is a pillar in our community and has blessed many with his dedication to the call of God on his life.

APOSTLE KIMBERLY DANIELS

As I have mentioned before, Apostle Kimberly is my spiritual mother. She is a modern-day Priscilla in my life. With her cutting edge in spiritual warfare and deliverance, she has taken my wife and me to new levels in God. Giving herself to intercession and the things of God has boomeranged into the lives of my family members. Her greatness is rooted in her connection with her husband, being a woman of great authority yet abiding under the covering of her spouse. Through her worldwide ministry and behind the scenes at home, she is an example as a spiritual and natural mother.

THELMA TYREE (MY MOTHER)

When I think of greatness, my mother, Thelma, is at the top of the list. She was a great mother. She raised three children as a single mom. She always provided for us, and if we had any hard times, we could not tell. We may not have worn Air Jordans or the most expensive brands, but she provided well. My mom moved us from a neighborhood of negative influence to live in a neighborhood where we could attend better schools and be involved in athletics. She was a woman who sacrificed everything for her children. She was the Proverbs 31 woman, the virtuous woman praised in the Bible. I love and salute this powerful woman who gave me life.

Fifteen

PHYSICAL AND SPIRITUAL DISCIPLINE (PART I)

I beseech you therefore, brethren, by the mercies of God, that you present your bodies a living sacrifice, holy, acceptable to God, which is your reasonable service.

—ROMANS 12:1

P hysical and spiritual discipline go together like a hand in a glove. Yoga, karate, and many other physical disciplines are founded in spirituality. It is no secret that meditation and belief in a higher power affect physical ability. Most massage therapists frequently use a method of healing the body called *Reiki*, which is based on metaphysics and is a teaching from the New Age movement. I mention this example to identify the connection between physical and spiritual discipline.

This chapter relates physical training to spirituality. I include prayer and meditation in my training. I do not open my spirit to any form of spirituality outside the teachings of the gospel of Jesus Christ. I am not closed-minded, just faithful to my God. I often say, "I do not do yoga; I do Jehovah!"

Spiritual Discipline

For this is the love of God, that we keep His commandments. And His commandments are not burdensome.

—1 John 5:3

Discipline is a bad word to many people. The key to discipline
is in the root word *disciple*. To be a disciple, a person must be
a follower of something or someone in whom they believe. It is
crazy to say that we do not have to believe in anything. Even
believing in nothing is a belief. We cannot get around it; we were
created to believe.

Discipline takes faith! The foundation of my faith is to believe
in God. The fruit of this foundation is having the ability to
believe in what I am trying to achieve. It's a dangerous practice to believe in God but not believe in the work that He does
through us. This statement summarizes what I am saying: *Have
faith in God and in what He wants to do through you!*

Spiritual discipline is not the same thing as following religious
rules and regulations. Trying to "be religious" can be boring,
burdensome, and repetitious. True spiritual discipline edifies the
spirit, body, and mind.

God is not a taskmaster holding in His hands a checklist of
what we are supposed to do every day. Spiritual discipline is
fulfilling when it is based on a relationship with Jesus Christ that
brings forth fruit. On the other hand, rules you follow to try to
force yourself to be disciplined become just hard work. Spending
time with God and getting to know Him takes the work out of
the relationship. Getting to know God makes you fall in love
with Him. When you fall in love with God, obeying Him is not
a *burden* but a *blessing.*

Think about when a man falls in love with a woman. When it is time for him to be with her, he does not complain, "I don't feel like meeting with her right now!" No, he is so full of excitement that he cannot wait to see her. The time they spend together can never be enough. This is what the Bible means when it says that the commandments of the Lord are not burdensome. We can easily accomplish things when the affections of our heart are set toward them.

I fell in love with God four years ago. The love that I have for him takes priority over everything in my life. This is what it means to give your life to Christ. He wants to be first in our hearts. I often ask people, "What is the last thing that you think about when you go to sleep at night and the first thing you think about when you wake up in the morning?" Whatever this thing on your mind may be, you can be assured that it is the closest and dearest thing to your heart.

My relationship with God comes before my wife, family, career, and everything else that concerns me. God showed me early in my walk with Him that if I put Him first, everything else in my life will fall into place. He is the center of my joy, and everything must be built around Him!

Putting God first, even before my wife, is the only way that I can love her like God commanded me to. If I put her first, she would be an idol in my life. Having her as an idol, I could never love her the way God really calls a man to love a woman, "just as Christ also loved the church and gave Himself for her" (Eph. 5:25), in Paul's words. Without being connected first to the love that God has for us, I cannot begin to love Leilah. It is the love that I have for God that stirs my heart to be faithful to my wife. Because I have been delivered from unfaithfulness, my wife does not mind me putting God first. When I did not put Him first in my life, I slept around with other women under no conviction. The love that Christ has for the church is what convicts me to be a husband of one wife. Obeying God is not a burden, and loving my beautiful wife and the mother of my children is not a burden.

My wife and I understand that it is a sin for us to put each other before God. We know that we have to give our children to God, and even they cannot come before Him. This may be hard for many people to figure out. It is simple to me—God said He would not have any person, place, or thing before Him. I do not attempt to figure it out, and I definitely did not make the rules. These are the commandments of God; I just follow them! This is what disciples do—they follow in utmost obedience.

When we approach spiritual discipline the right way, it will cause us to get rid of old destructive habits and create new life-giving ones. Habits aren't always bad! Let's take a look at habits from the positive side. *There is such a thing as a good habit.*

Whether you are dealing with spiritual or physical matters, it is important to know this: if there is no *pain*, there is no *gain*. To be honest, getting up in the wee hours of the morning to pray is not exactly easy. Turning a favorite television show off to read the Bible can also be a challenge. Thinking on things that edify your spirit and do not gratify your flesh can also be an obstacle that's hard to get over. Despite all of these things, I have good news—disciplines like these are attainable! Here are some ways to see them bear fruit.

BE A DISCIPLE OF THE VISION.

Formulate a plan and follow it. It may not be easy at first, but do not be afraid to start small and build from there. It is very important to know where you are and where you need to begin. I can remember putting more weight on my shoulders than I could carry, and I ended up getting frustrated. I had to start over with what was comfortable for my circumstances at the time. Be realistic with yourself and take it step by step. You need to see results. Results mean everything! It can be very discouraging to work hard and see no results. This is why most people get frustrated and give up. Results give you incentives to keep working hard.

FAST WHEN GOD LEADS YOU TO FAST.

It is important to have balance and be led by the Lord in spiritual discipline. An example of this is fasting. When considering whether to fast, let God lead you. Isaiah 58:5 asks a question that we should also ask: "Is this the fast that [God has] chosen?" It would not be wise for a pregnant woman to do a fast that would deprive her baby of nutrients needed. It also would not be smart for a football player to fast during training camp in 100-degree weather when he is practicing twice a day. But there are other times when it can be a great part of spiritual discipline

If we allow God to choose the fast in His timing, it will be spiritually and physically successful. Not that it's easy to do—I will be the first to admit that my biggest challenge in spiritual discipline is fasting. I am praying for God to help me in that area.

COMMAND THE MORNING.

This is the habit I mentioned earlier when I wrote about Mickey the cat, my mother's faithful companion, and how he gets up every morning with my spiritual mom to have time with God. Spending time with God is one of my most fruitful spiritual disciplines. Commanding the morning is based on Job 38:12–13:

> Have you commanded the morning since your days
>   began,
> And caused the dawn to know its place,
> That it might take hold of the ends of the earth
> And the wicked be shaken out of it?

I was introduced to the principle about a year ago, and I became a commander of the morning at the beginning of the 2007 season. I command my mornings through prayer with a group of intercessors on a prayer line. Some of the lines have up to ninety people praying on conference lines. My prayer group has no more than five to seven intercessors at a time on the line. Apostles Ardell and Kimberly Daniels head the vision for these prayer lines.

We have professional football players, famous gospel singers, businessmen, movie stars, and a variety of people from all aspects of life on these lines. I like the close-knit relationship between the people on my line. It is so interesting to pray with people whom you have never met before. I often imagine what they look like until meeting them. It is good to be able to put a face with a voice after actually meeting some of the intercessors.

After my first few weeks on the line, it became clear to me that getting up at 5:00 a.m. to pray did not fit into my practice schedule. Rest was more important to me at the time. I told Apostle Kimberly that it was difficult for me to command the morning and be fresh at practice.

She told me, "You play football, and we will command the morning for you. You can spend time with the Lord in your free time." It is important to have balance and be led by the Lord in spiritual discipline.

When I injured my wrist at the beginning of the season, I took advantage of the situation and started commanding the morning again. I received a better understanding of what this principle of prayer was about at the time. Commanding the morning consists of getting up early in the morning to take authority over the third prayer watch (3:00 a.m. to 6:00 a.m.). There were three prayer watches in the Old Testament and four watches in the New Testament. The Bible says that Jesus prayed on the fourth watch.

The root purpose of commanding the morning is to get up early to declare the will of God for our day. By doing this, we overturn and cancel any negativity that may have stirred during the night. The Bible says that we can take hold of the corners of the earth through prayer and shake darkness out of it. We release light in the wee hours of the morning that establishes our day.

This discipline ignited my heart with faith. It did not matter if obstacles occurred throughout the day because I had already talked to God about them. When light comes, darkness must flee! By the time the sun shone, it was my friend and not my enemy. When I command the morning, I can honestly say that I do not worry about tomorrow because every day in my life is established.

If you want to know more about commanding the morning, you can read *Give It Back!* by Kimberly Daniels. This book gives Scripture references concerning commanding the morning. It also shares testimonies of the great things that have happened through this kind of prayer.

The following prayer is a sneak preview from *Give It Back!* I encourage you to join the Commander of the Morning program with us! Here are some suggestions as you pray this prayer and step out on faith:[1]

- Start out by reading this prayer verbatim.
- As you research the Scriptures and develop an understanding of why you are praying, begin to use your own words to expound what you have read through your prayer.
- List your prayer "targets" (people, situations, needs, worries—anything on your heart) before you begin praying. The Commander of the Morning leader will also give you some prayer points each week.
- Be prepared for prophetic insight from God as you pray, and make a listing of them to use in your prayer time. (You'll want to have a pen and paper available.)
- Contact us to become part of an intercessors group, or e-mail morningcommander@kimberly daniels.com for testimonies, revelations, and comments.

COMMANDER OF THE MORNING PRAYER

Father God, in the name of Jesus, I rise early to declare Your lordship! I get under the covering and anointing of the early riser. I come in agreement with the heavens to declare Your glory! Lord, release the mysteries unto me to bring heaven down to Earth. The stars (chief angels) are battling on my behalf ahead of time.

My appointed times have been set by God in the heavens. I declare spermatic words that will make contact with the womb of the morning and make her pregnant. At sunrise the dawn will give birth to the will of God, and light will shine on wickedness to shake it from the heavens. At twilight my enemies will flee, and newly found spoils will await me at my destination. My destiny is inevitable!

O God, let my prayers meet You this morning. I command the morning to open its ears unto me and hear my cry. Let conception take place that prayer will rain down and be dispatched upon the earth to do Your will.

I command the earth to get in place to receive heavenly instructions on my behalf. My lands are subdued. I command all the elements of creation to take heed and obey! As my praise resounds and the day breaks, the earth shall yield her increase unto me. I declare that the first light has come!

The firstfruit of my morning is holy, and the entire day will be holy. I prophesy the will of God to the morning so that the dayspring (dawn) will know its place in my days. I decree that the first light will shake wickedness from the four corners of the earth. The lines (my portion) are fallen on my behalf in pleasant (sweet, agreeable) places, and I have a secure heritage.

I am strategically lined up with the ladder that touches the third heaven and sits on Earth. The angels are descending and ascending according to the words that I speak. Whatever I bind or loose on Earth is already bound or loosed in heaven. Revelation, healing, deliver-

ance, salvation, peace, joy, relationships, finances, and resources that have been demonically blocked are being loosed unto me now! What is being released unto me is transferring to every person that I associate myself with. I am contagiously blessed!

As I command the morning and capture the day, time is being redeemed. The people of God have taken authority over the fourth watch of the day. The spiritual airways and highways are being hijacked for Jesus. The atmosphere of the airways over me, my family, my church, my community, my city, my state, my nation, and the world is producing a new climate. This new climate is constructing a godly stronghold in times of trouble. The thinking of people will be conducive to the agenda of the kingdom of heaven.

Every demonic agenda or evil thought pattern designed against the agenda of the kingdom of heaven is destroyed at the root of conception, in Jesus's name! I come into agreement with the saints—as we have suffered violence, we take by force! No longer will we accept anything that is dealt unto us in our days. I declare that the kingdom has come, and the will of God will be done on Earth as it is in heaven.

As the sun rises today, let it shine favorably upon the people and the purposes of God. Daily destiny is my portion because I have no thought for tomorrow. I am riding on the wings of the morning into a new day of victory. God, You separated the night and the day to declare my days, years, and seasons. I am the light of the earth, and I have been separated from darkness. This light declares my destiny!

The Lord has given me dominion over the elements and all the work of His hands. He has placed them under my feet. Because I fear the name of the Lord, the Sun of Righteousness shall arise with healing in His wings, and I shall tread down the wicked until they become ashes under my feet. I commit to walk in this dominion daily. I decree and declare a new day, a new season, and a fresh anointing. As the ordinances of the constellation have received orders from God on my behalf, they shall manifest in the earth realm. The ingredients of my destiny are programmed into my days, years, and seasons. I bind every force that would attempt to capture my destiny illegitimately.

I plead the blood of Jesus over every principality, power, ruler of darkness, and spiritual wickedness in high places assigned against my purpose. I bind every destiny pirate, destiny thief, and destiny devourer in the name of Jesus! They are dethroned and dismantled and have no influence over my days. Every curse sent against my days is reversed and boomeranged back to the pits of hell. I displace the Luciferian spirit.

I bind every false light-bearer and counterfeit son of the morning. My prayers will disrupt dark plans and give my enemies a nonprosperous day. I have victory over my enemies every morning. Because I obey the Lord and serve Him, my days will prosper! This is the day that the Lord has made, and I will rejoice and be glad in it! Amen.[2]

SCRIPTURE REFERENCES FOR COMMANDER
OF THE MORNING PRAYER

They [Deborah and Barak] fought from the heavens;
The stars [princes] from their courses [heavenly path-
ways] fought against Sisera.

—Judges 5:20

Have you commanded the morning since your days
began,
And caused the dawn to know its place,
That it might take hold of the ends of the earth
And the wicked be shaken out of it?

—Job 38:12–13

They [the lepers] rose at twilight [the light between night
and sunrise] to go to the camp of the Syrians;...Therefore
they [the Syrians] arose and fled at twilight, and left the
camp intact—their tents, their horses, and their donkeys
[and all their spoils]—and they fled for their lives.

—2 Kings 7:5, 7

But to You I have cried out, O LORD,
And in the morning my prayer comes before You.

—Psalm 88:13

The lines [inheritance or lot in life] have fallen to me in
pleasant [sweet, agreeable] places;
Yes, I have a goodly [legitimate and conforming to the
established rules that God has laid out for me in the
heavens] heritage.

—Psalm 16:6

Then he [Jacob] dreamed, and behold, a ladder was set up on the earth, and its top reached to [the third] heaven; and there the angels of God were ascending and descending on it.

—Genesis 28:12

If I take the wings of the morning [the pinnacle or highest point of the morning]...

—Psalm 139:9

This is the way of those who are foolish...
The upright shall have dominion over them in the morning.

—Psalm 49:13–14

I rise before the dawning of the morning,
And cry for help;
I hope in Your word.
My eyes are awake through the night watches,
That I may meditate on Your word.

—Psalm 119:147–148

You are all sons of light and sons of the day.

—1 Thessalonians 5:5

This is the day the LORD has made;
We will rejoice and be glad in it.

—Psalm 118:24

May these verses and my challenge build a fire in your heart to become a Commander of the Morning!

Sixteen

PHYSICAL AND SPIRITUAL
DISCIPLINE (PART 2)

W e would have to spend less time praying for healing if we would eat and exercise properly. The Bible instructs us about everything that we need in life. God wants His people to be physically as well as spiritually fit. I said it earlier, and I will say it again: *results matter!* Many people get discouraged with their exercise programs because they do not experience results right away. God gives us a remedy in His Word for being discouraged due to a lack of results:

> For we walk by *faith*, not by sight.
> —2 Corinthians 5:7, emphasis added

There is such a thing as "being between results." This is when you need 2 Corinthians 5:7 to put gas in your tank to press on. Eventually you will see results! In choosing a workout, you must start out at a place that challenges you. Remember, no pain, no gain! You do not necessarily have to do suicide laps or run stadium steps, but you must do a workout that brings you out of your comfort zone. Whether you are attempting to establish good habits in spiritual discipline or in physical discipline, your flesh is lazy. It will make excuses and try to take the easy way out.

Do yourself a favor and do not listen to the voice of your flesh. Listen to that small soft voice on the inside of you that tells you to do the right thing. Your flesh will speak louder than your spirit and will even try to drown out that small voice. Be strong and listen to the right voice, the one that speaks truth, and you'll be on the road to fitness.

Keep in mind the importance of rest. I have known many athletically inclined people who periodically take a break from exercise. Even if they do not exercise for long periods of time, when they work out again, their bodies respond to workouts faster than others. This is called *muscle memory*. Your muscles can remember the great time they had working out and respond accordingly.

Think of this principle in regard to spiritual memory too. If a person has fallen off in his or her prayer time or in reading the Bible, if they get back into the swing of things with God, they'll find they have *Holy Ghost muscle memory*!

No matter what kind of spiritual or physical fitness program you are in today, this day can be a new day for the new you! You can apply these spiritual principles from God to your workout plan and do great. Workouts can be greater than us and hard to accomplish. This is why you need to depend on someone greater than you to coach you through.

God wants to be involved in every part of your life. I include Him in everything I do. He is my Lord of lords and Coach of coaches! There is nothing like being drilled in physical discipline by the Word of God. If you are out of shape or overweight and have tried every plan, now is the time to try God's plan. He has a master plan for our physical bodies. He created them! The Word of God has so much to say about being physically whole and healthy.

—◆—

My spiritual mom was a world-class sprinter and trained and studied under a lot of European coaches. Her son Michael wanted to go into the NFL, but she did not know anything about football at the time. She went to school at Florida State University on a track and field scholarship. She was so uninterested in football that she never attended one football game during her entire time in college. She purchased a Madden video game so that her son could learn the rules of the game. She also gave him track workouts and trained him to get in shape for the NFL. Her son was in such great physical shape that the participants in Jerry Rice's football training camp could not keep up with him. Today he is a wide receiver for the New York Giants. He never played football in college and only played a little during high school.

She was also the fastest sprinter in the military. She worked in military gymnasiums around the world during her tour in the army. She led battalions in physical training in the morning and helped the soldier's wives to get in shape in the evenings. During one of the conferences she sponsored, she had a physical training class called "The War Against Fat." Two hundred women and a few men met her at 6:00 a.m., and she taught them a workout plan, specializing in circuit training. She gave the group a workout plan like the one I have listed below. As a result of that one class, one man in attendance lost 100 pounds in six months. Two other ladies lost 60 and 40 pounds in less than six months.

It is my honor to share her fitness plan in this chapter.[1]

Doing Territorial Warfare on Your Body
—Kimberly Daniels

As we start, let's be realistic. Not everyone is going to have a "six-pack." However, you can get your abdominal area in better shape than it is now. You may even end up with a "four-pack or a five-pack," but surely God does not require you to have a cooler full.

Let's attack that midsection with the Word of God. (Remember: the Scriptures are just as important as the exercises!)

1. Abdominal siege

Upper Abs Crunch Reach—Philippians 3:14

I press toward the goal for the prize of the upward call of God in Christ Jesus.

Position yourself flat on your back. Fold your hands behind your head with your elbows being parallel to the ground. Bend your knees with your feet flat on the floor. Begin your crunch exercise by reaching your hands straight out before you as you lift your torso up. As you lie back down at the completion of a crunch, bring your hands behind your head again. Start the exercise over. Start by doing a number of crunch reaches that are attainable but challenging for the level of fitness you are at. As you do this exercise, think about what your goals are in life, reaching for them with every repetition. Do this as you are reaching ahead, and forget the things that are behind you, according to the exercise scripture.

Lower Abs Flutter Kicks—Proverbs 16:11

Honest weights and scales are the LORD's; all the weights in the bag are His work.

Position yourself on your back with your legs barely extended off the floor. Your hands should be folded behind your head. Balancing the weight of holding your legs in the air, begin to kick your legs in and out, bringing your knees toward your chest. As you are balancing your legs in the air, think on the scripture that says, "Honest weights and scales are the LORD's."

Obliques Quickening Turns—John 6:63

It is the Spirit who gives life; the flesh profits nothing.

Stand with your legs spread a comfortable length apart. Hold a dumbbell (choose the weight of your own discretion) in each hand. Hold the dumbbells to your midsection. Twist your body from side to side at approximately at a 90-degree angle. The pace must be fast. Choose the number of twists per set, and compete three sets with full recovery between each set. Full recovery is important to get the ultimate workout with each set. Meditate on the Spirit of God quickening your flesh to do well at this exercise. Meditate on the fact that there is no profit in the flesh. Allow the Lord to quicken it and cause it to respond to His holy Word!

Transverse (Abdominis) Tummy Hold—Hebrews 10:23

Let us hold fast the confession of our hope without wavering, for He who promised is faithful.

Position yourself on your hands and knees. Bridge yourself up with your upper body leaning on your elbows. Push yourself up on your toes and hold your tummy in as tight as you can. Your body should be straight like a board. Imagine yourself trying to push your stomach through your back. Start out by holding your stomach in for twenty seconds. If this is not a challenge to you, increase it in ten-second segments. Decrease your seconds by five if twenty seconds is too difficult. As you do this exercise, you will be able to hold your stomach in for longer periods of time. Remember to meditate on your exercise scripture as you work out. Think on whatever you are holding on to as a profession of faith.

Abdominal Traditional Sit-ups—Proverbs 24:16

For a righteous man may fall seven times and rise again.

You will need to secure your feet in some manner. You can use a partner or exercise equipment, or you can put your feet under a piece of furniture at your home that is strong enough to hold your weight. Put your hands behind your head with your elbows parallel to the ground. As you sit up, slightly turn your body, touching your right elbow to the left knee. Switch and touch the left elbow to the right knee. Continue to alternate throughout the exercise. The faster your momentum is in this exercise, the better the results you will receive. Find the right number of repetitions for you and complete three sets. While meditating on your scripture, focus on rising up. Press your way up as you rise and think on all the things that you have risen out of and will rise from, in Jesus's name!

2. UPPER BODY TRAINING

Upper Arms Dumbbell Run—1 Timothy 6:11

But you, O man of God, flee these things and pursue righteousness, godliness, faith, love, patience, gentleness.

Stand with a dumbbell in each hand. Choose the weight of your dumbbell. Set yourself in a standing set position as if you were about to start a race. Put one hand in a forward position high in the air and the other hand behind you with your elbow bent as if you are about to run. You should be in a position as if you are about to swing your arms while running.

Standing still, swing your arms as if you are running. Maintain good form, keeping your lower back tight and your legs still. Look straight ahead and be focused as if you are really running. Do the amount of repetitions you feel like you can start at, and do three sets. Make sure you are working out. Do not cheat yourself! Imagine that you are fleeing from ungodliness and running toward the things of God.

Shoulder Area Strongholds—2 Corinthians 10:4–5

For the weapons of our warfare are not carnal but mighty in God for pulling down strongholds, casting down arguments and every high thing that exalts itself against the knowledge of God.

Stand on your feet with a dumbbell in each hand. Raise your hands over your head with your elbows locked. You body should be straight from your hands to the floor. Pull the dumbbells down to your shoulders and push them back up again. Do the number of repetitions you choose to start at. Complete three sets. As you pull the dumbbells down, think on the strongholds that God wants you to deal with during your workout.

3. LOWER BODY TRAINING

Thighs and Buttocks Duck Squats—Exodus 1:12

But the more they afflicted them, the more they multiplied and grew.

Stand and spread your feet at a comfortable position. Squat as if you are in a weight room doing squats with weights. Look straight ahead, and imagine yourself sitting in a duck position in your squat. Keep your lower back tight. You do not need dumbbells, but you may use them if you like. Use heavier dumbbells than usual for this exercise if you choose to use them. From the duck-squat position, imagine a million pounds on your shoulders and push upward with force. Come back to your duck-squat position and push up again. Start at twenty-five to forty repetitions, and complete three sets. Think about the things that have tried to hold you down and rise up above them.

EXTRA: BED-ABS

You can do this exercise before you get out of the bed in the morning. Point your toes straight up (with heels on the bed), and reach for your toes with your fingers extended; slightly lift your back from the bed (your body should be making an *L* shape—with your arms pointed straight ahead, parallel to the bed). Once you are in position, hold your stomach tight and count for twenty to fifty repetitions. The number of repetitions varies according to the individual. Do three to four sets every morning before getting out of bed. This exercise is great after you command your morning!

CREATING AN EXERCISE CIRCUIT

Create an exercise circuit from the exercises listed earlier. To create an exercise circuit, you must set up exercise stations in a room with open space. For example, one station may be for jumping rope, and another station may be for doing sit-ups and other lying-down exercises such as leg lifts. Other exercises that you can do at a station are:

- Push-ups
- Riding a bike
- Running on a treadmill
- Running in place
- Lunges
- Bunny hops

You will need a stopwatch or someone to time you. Set your goals for each station. For example, you may set a goal of doing twenty push-ups at a station. Some of your goals may be set by time. This means you can jump rope for two minutes instead of doing repetitions. After you have set goals for each station, you are ready to start your circuit training!

Complete one circuit without a break between exercises, and then rest for three to five minutes afterward. After your rest, check your pulse, and start the next circuit if your pulse is normal. If it is not normal, take enough extra minutes of rest to get it down to where it needs to be. Do a total of three circuits to complete your workout. The scripture to meditate on while doing your circuit is

2 Timothy 4:7: "I have fought the good fight, I have finished the race, I have kept the faith."

When doing your circuit, focus on finishing it. Keep the faith and you will finish! Be faithful to do your circuits at least three times a week, and not only will you lose weight, but your body will also tone up. Alternating workout days gives your body time to recover. Your stomach and calf muscles can be worked daily as long as you stretch them properly. It is important to warm up and stretch at least thirty minutes before this workout. You can determine if you are warmed up when you break a sweat. (This may not be applicable to some people who do not sweat easily.)

Cooling down is also necessary after a good workout. Jogging in place, riding a bike, or walking on a treadmill for fifteen to twenty minutes are great cool-down exercises. No matter how hot the temperature is, wear a windbreaker or sweat suit when warming up or cooling down. Warming up, cooling down, and dressing properly are preventive maintenance against injuries.

You Have a Right to Eat as Long as You Eat Right!

Most dieters...die eating! For me, diet is a bad word because it focuses on abstaining. And it's no fun! Life is miserable without enjoying your food. How would you like to lose weight by eating right and have fun doing it? I know this sounds impossible, but you can't knock it until you try it.

Meal tips

- Drink protein smoothies to curb your appetite.
  Smoothies are fun! You can even make your own
  smoothies. Use fresh fruit, 1 cup of nonfat fruit

yogurt, and the fruit juice of your choice. Blend it
with ice chips in your blender. It tastes great!

- Drink 8 ounces of water four to six times a day.
- Eat four to six small meals per day (including
  snacks). By doing this you will meet your body's
  need to consume food. It is important that we eat
  and not neglect our body of its right to eat, as long
  as we eat right.
- You may eat all the raw fresh vegetables you like.
- Eat walnuts and raisins for snacks. Walnuts have
  been proven to fight fat.

Your body has a right to eat. Starving your body is not only
miserable but also dangerous! Eating the right foods makes your
eating discipline a delight.

Avoid foods that put you territorially "out of place." White
breads, potatoes, pastas, ham, and pork will distract you from
your goal. Also avoid both diet sodas and regular sodas.

As you experience results, you may treat yourself to an
"anything-you-want-to-eat day." As you get results, you may find
you don't want to eat just anything. You will find yourself being
more disciplined about what you eat.

I do not claim to be a nutritionist, but these are foods that
have especially blessed me. I pray that they bless you too.

- Fresh vegetables (raw)
- Celery and carrot sticks with dressing of choice
- Tomatoes and okra
- Vegetables (cooked)
- Fresh beans (cooked)
- Brown rice

- Honey-wheat breads
- Raisins
- Walnuts
- Chicken (baked)
- Fish (baked)
- Lean meats
- Whole-wheat pitas
- Turkey
- Turkey bacon
- Turkey sausage
- Canned beets
- Salads (with chicken)
- Romaine lettuce
- Olive oil (in cooking)
- Lean beef
- Fruits (especially melons and berries)
- Pink grapefruit
- Fruit yogurt (especially nonfat)
- Tortillas and salsa
- Boiled eggs

Do your own research on foods that burn fat. Make sure you get enough protein in your meals because it builds muscle mass.

If you eat the right foods, you can literally lose weight while you sleep. Now that's the kind of warfare I like!

Please do not give up easily. This program may be difficult for you at first, but after you get past the first few weeks, it gets easier. Also, remember that too much of anything is not good for anybody. Eating overly large portions of food takes away from the purpose of working out. I pray that as you determine to work out and eat right, the Lord will give you moderation in eating your meals. As you begin to eat less, your stomach will get the idea and shrink in size. I do not believe in luck, so be blessed!

———∿∿———

I pray that I have stirred you up about getting in shape and caused you to get serious about being spiritually and physically fit. By doing so you will live longer, feel better, and please God! As you are doing territorial warfare on each part of your body, meditate on the promises of God. You may want to also include praise and worship music as a part of the workout.

A couple words of warning: do not get territorially out of place by checking your weight on a scale or counting calories religiously! If you have done these, you know that they don't really work. Counting calories is a drag!

You may weigh yourself periodically, but do not get obsessed with it. You may be losing fat, and the scale cannot detect your progress. Losing inches is a clear sign of progress.

People sometimes get discouraged because they don't experience results. Being able to recognize results has a lot to do with your *attitude*. Begin to see yourself as you want to look, and do not forget to get rid of the word *diet*. Think of diet as a demon. Refer to your war against fat as a *fitness program*.

Finally, be realistic. It takes a person a long time to get out of shape, and getting in shape does not happen overnight. God takes us from one glory to the next. Let's praise Him along the way! The Bible says that we should enter into His gates with thanksgiving. Enter the gates of your workout with a thankful heart. Begin to see things that are not (your body in its shape right now) as though they are. Do not focus on what you have to lose. Focus on what you have to gain! You are not just losing weight but gaining a healthy body. Your goal should not be just to lose weight but to be toned. Ultimately, you want to eat the right foods and do the right exercises to promote proper muscle mass.

It is my prayer that you will be all that God has called you to be and that you will walk in the anointing of the *new you*! Wage war on fat and hate it. You can be both a demon-buster and a fat-buster as you walk in the anointing of being spiritually and physically fit.

Seventeen

DREAMS AND DESTINY

But without faith it is impossible to please Him, for he who comes to God must believe that He is, and that He is a rewarder of those who diligently seek Him.

—Hebrews 11:6

I thank God for the opportunity to walk you through my life. I have shared some moments that are dearest to my heart. The opportunity to share my Super Bowl dream is a blessing. The overflow of this experience has changed my life forever. One play has opened so many doors. Besides that cover of *Sports Illustrated* that featured me, I was invited to be a guest on the Ellen DeGeneres and Jimmy Kimmel shows. ESPN highlighted my story on *First Take*, the *Jim Rome Is Burning* show, and *Outside the Lines*. I was honored to give my testimony on TBN and *The 700 Club*. I have also appeared on NBC and Fox networks.

Since the beginning of my career, I have waited to see my jersey in the local athletic stores. Not long ago as I was signing autographs in Circuit City, it was hard for me to contain myself.

When I think of where I have come from and realize that only the Lord could have done this thing, it gets overwhelming.

The icing on the cake was when I stood to receive the key to New York City with my teammates. What an awesome honor! Most of the players agree that the excitement of the parade down the streets of New York City was more electrifying than the Super Bowl itself. The estimated two million participants created a crowd that looked like a sea of people. Whoopi Goldberg hosted the occasion for the television viewers. We were on parade before the world. I looked into the crowd to see if I could recognize anyone I knew, but there were so many faces it was impossible to do.

The fact that I was a homeboy from around the corner made the feeling even greater. I was proud to be a New York Giant, proud to be from New Jersey, and proud to be in America where things like this could happen to a regular person like me.

After the parade we had the pep rally of pep rallies. In my book, there is nothing like New York Giants fans. They filled the stadium. The dark cloud of controversy and uncertainty that ruled over our team had floated away, and the sun was shining bright. The light had come! As I looked on the faces of Coach Coughlin and Eli Manning, I saw relief and joy. The once ridiculed defensive players, now considered the best in the world, joked around with each other as they enjoyed the moment. Everything had taken a turn for the best. We were one team with one vision that turned into one victory that caused us to experience the manifestation of the same dream—a dream that none of us will ever have to wake up from.

THE PLACE OF DREAMS AND VISIONS IN DESTINY

Dreams do come true! I know they do because I have not only seen them come true, but I have also *experienced* them coming true. I have always marveled when people tell me about vivid dreams they have had, because I rarely have dreams. I covet to have dreams and see visions.

I have often joked with people about asking God to allow me to see angels. When you think of angels, do you think of light creatures dressed in robes floating in the air? The dream I had about the injuries on my team was so different from that idea. It was clear, specific, and dark. It was real. Even though I do not have many dreams, the ones I have are meaningful.

I have known people who live what is going to happen in their lives in their dreams, and in some ways their dream life is more real to them than their waking one. My wife's mother, Bugadis, is a dreamer. She always dreams about my wife being pregnant before we ever get the news. She has never been wrong. Four days before the Super Bowl, Coach Aleem called and told me that he dreamed that I would have the greatest game of my life. This was really a prophetic dream.

God speaks through dreams and visions, and the more real dreams are to a person, the more real God can be to them. My cousin Rachael had a near-death experience and went to heaven in a dream. She told me she saw my mother dancing and being joyful in heaven. Sometimes the Lord allows us to get a glimpse of glory, such as Rachael's, to comfort our hearts. As much as I desperately miss my mother, my cousin's dream brought me a bit of comfort.

There are people who may be quick to criticize me for saying that God was involved in what happened at the Super Bowl. In no way am I saying that God loves the Giants more than He loves the Patriots! I am saying that sometimes God has to cause a game to be won to fulfill a dream. I believe that so many promises and dreams were fulfilled for so many people at the end of this game.

God did not just do His mighty work for David Tyree alone—others were also greatly blessed! I do have the responsibility to make my personal blessing known and give Him all the glory—as if He did it just for me! God is so much bigger than a Super Bowl game. On the other hand, I thank Him for being that big and getting involved in the simple matters of my life.

When I returned from the Super Bowl, I received two dreams that were dated days before the game. Check them out:

DREAM #1 (JANUARY 22, 2008—FROM AN INTERCESSOR)

> I dreamed that I went to a place that looked like a football stadium. It was a multilevel facility. I was sitting in a stadium box looking down, but the place was really like an atrium. I exited the stadium and saw people getting into cars. For some reason I decided to stay with the crowd that was gathering outside of the stadium. I was standing in a large crowd with familiar faces. All of a sudden, someone said, "Is that Michael Jennings?" Mike was standing there with a number 15 jersey on. Then the scene turned into a street pep rally. The crowd was dancing from left to right, and Mike was in the middle of the crowd. The crowd was rapping, "Mike can do it; throw the ball to him!" Everybody was dancing around Mike.

DREAM #2 (JANUARY 29, 2008)

Mike (Michael Jennings) and a football team were in a room. It appeared to be a room where you plan things. It was similar to a locker room, but it had a conference table in the middle of it. All the players were sitting around the table. I could not hear what they were talking about, but I remember Mike saying, "We are going to have to take this." The men responded, "Take it with what? We ain't got no power." As he is pulling this huge machine gun out of a gym bag, Mike says, "Oh, I got some power!" You could see the white of all the football players' eyes. It was crazy because Mike had on a black do-rag, and he had scars on his neck. The next thing that I remember is that the players are running out of a store pushing baskets full of stuff. Mike was in the rear with the machine gun held high in the air. He was walking as if to say, "Please make me use this—'cause I know how." The owners ran out of the store behind the players, saying, "We've been robbed! We've been robbed!" The scene switched to the New England Patriots, and they were saying, "We've been robbed." They said, "To come all this way and be taken out at the end is highway robbery!"

The symbols in these dreams are so significant. My good friend and Christian brother Michael Jennings, number 15, is a wide receiver on the New York Giants team. I believe that the fact that my rookie number was 15 is also relevant.

Sometimes dreams can be interpreted in types. For some reason God used Michael Jennings in the dream to represent me. The first dream depicted everything that happened at the victory parade in New York. The second dream represented what happened at the Super Bowl. This dream foretold the upset before it ever happened.

I believe the reason for these dreams occurring before the Super Bowl even happened is this: God did not want any "ifs, ands, or buts" concerning His involvement in that day. Yes, the Super Bowl was definitely a God thing!

Eighteen

FROM MY HEART TO YOU

W hen I think back to how God has worked in my life, I thank Him for so many things. I made it out of college without becoming a statistic. I thank Him for protecting me and keeping me out of all the traps that young blacks can fall into. Finishing college is a great achievement for a young black man.

Statistics concerning black men in America are scary. In 2001, statistics showed that 32 percent of black men in America will enter state or federal prison at some time.[1] The number of black men in jail or prison has grown fivefold in the past twenty years. It has gotten so bad that more black men are behind bars than are enrolled in colleges or universities, according to recent studies. A study found that in 2000 there were 791,600 black men in jail or prison, and 603,032 were enrolled in colleges or universities. By contrast, the study said that in 1980, 143,000 African American men were in jail or prison while 463,700 were enrolled in colleges or universities.[2]

It is also interesting to know that studies indicate that the reason that the number of black men in jail or prison is climbing so rapidly is because of drug-related crimes. Statistics show that 50 percent of inmates are in prison or jail because they were under the influence of drugs or alcohol.[3]

As I look at these statistics I cannot help but say, "It could have been me!" God gave me so many second chances in life. Alcohol and drugs could have made me another statistic. Every time I blacked out and woke up not knowing where I was, God kept me. I could have been another brother on death row. The curse of being an alcoholic came down through generations in my family, but it has been stopped now. People often think that only "bad people" end up with sentences like life in prison or on death row. I know that people in situations like this are not always bad. They just make bad decisions and end up in the wrong place, at the wrong time, doing the wrong thing, with the wrong people.

I am not ignorant of the fact that in regard to black men, the number of black men in prison is not just a problem—it is an epidemic! Statistics have shown that in 2001 an estimated 2.7 percent of adults served time in prison in America.[4] Racial statistics are as follows:

- Black males—16.6 percent
- Hispanic males—7.7 percent
- White males—2.6 percent[5]

There is a serious problem with the destinies of black males in this country, and it cannot be overlooked. I should have rightfully been a part of the numbers above. It was only God's mercy and grace that spared my life. I hope you have a better understanding of why I love Jesus and why I don't hesitate to give Him all the honor, glory, and praise for everything I've achieved in my life.

I would like to shout out to all my brothers—white, black, or any other race—who are incarcerated and who read this book:

Jesus loves you, brother! He has a mighty army of prayer warriors interceding for you. Whatever you may be locked down for in the natural does not have to lock you down in the spirit. You can be free in Jesus, even if you are in prison. I am not offering you another "jailhouse religion" but a relationship with Christ that will make you free indeed. It is not too late for you to give Him your heart today!

Pray this prayer with me:

> *Jesus, I repent for my sins and anything that I have done to make me end up where I am today. I draw from the anointing that is being released in my heart as I read this book. Jesus, I receive You as Lord. Help me to have a fresh start in life. I renounce all unforgiveness and bitterness. I become a part of the statistics of heaven and renounce the statistics of the system.*
>
> *I am a new creature in Christ Jesus. My old thoughts and ways are passing away as I allow the Word of God to renew my mind. Lord, connect me with the right people so that I can do the right thing. Holy Spirit, You move prevalently in the halls of prisons. Move for me in this place, and use me for Your glory. I decree that I am in this place but not of this place. The spirit of recidivism does not bind me, and You are the only one who can rehabilitate. Lord, as I submit my vessel to You, I am being raised up as Your soldier. What was meant for evil has been turned around for my good. God, You get the glory for every day that I spend locked up. I thank You for a supernatural deliverance from my situation and a release into Your perfect will. While You are moving for me, I want to be used by You! If You*

can use anybody…Lord, use me! In Jesus's name I pray.
Amen.

I encourage you to believe what you have just prayed. Just saying these words means nothing without faith. God has heard you, and as you continue to meditate on the Word of God, He will confirm your prayers. Connect with other believers around you, and be a strong force for the Lord. It is the mercy of God that I am not where you are now. I am confident that if you believe, God *will give you* the desires of your heart. May this book release faith that will manifest miracles in your heart and circumstances!

To the Next Generation

I am excited about what I believe God is doing in your generation. Knowing about the suicide, murder, incarceration, depression, and hopelessness that devour young people every day, I release strength to you. I pray that my testimony has touched your life. On behalf of all athletes of faith, I ask your forgiveness for the images of false success and the poor role models who have been put before you in the world we live in today. Many whom you have admired and looked up to have disappointed you with their sad endings in drugs, divorce, reckless living, and many other negative outcomes.

My heart is heavy because the Ten Commandments have been removed from the public arena and Bibles from schools. Actions like these have created a generation of young people who are insensitive to and ignorant of the things of God.

I am honored to let you know that you can serve God at a young age and love every minute of it. Do not let anyone trick you into thinking that you need to wait until you are older to get to know God. This book tells my story of the many mistakes I made as a young man. I believe that God gave me the opportunity to write my story so that you will not have to make some of the mistakes that I made.

Not every person who made the mistakes I made has had or will have a good ending. God wants you to have a happy ending, but all happy endings must begin somewhere.

You need to know this about me: I am not a religious person. What I am presenting to you is not about going to church or being a good person. Without God in our lives, none of us are good, and we all have problems.

I am presenting what I believe the answer is to all of your problems—and mine. It's Jesus Christ! I know that people have many forms of faith and ways that they worship God. I am inviting you to get to know my God. The way He commands me to worship Him is in spirit and in truth. Isn't that what it is all about anyway? Being real! God just wants you to come to Him just as you are and be real.

The world is hooked on reality shows. What happened to my life at the Super Bowl is reality, and it has been my honor to share it with you. I purpose to be up front and bold about my faith in God in hope that this boldness will become contagious and touch someone like you.

I believe that God is touching your heart right now. Do not be afraid to sell out to Him. You can be a lover and follower of Christ at a young age. Let's make Jesus the style!

This generation is already fired up about the supernatural. Why do you think Criss Angel is so popular on MTV? Young people are fascinated with the supernatural because there is something on the inside of all of us that desires to experience the real power of God.

My God is more than a building with pews, a choir, and a man wearing a priest's collar. I invite you to meet a God who can come into your life, introduce you to His power, and lead you into your destiny. Do not be afraid to dream big dreams. But more than that, you need to get to know the One who is the Maker of dreams!

I speak life into your destiny. I pray that you'll be protected against drug addiction, rebellion, premarital sex, teen pregnancy, and all other potentially fatal distractions. These things are ungodly and do not make sense apart from God. They all lead to dead-end roads that will take you off the course of your destiny. Even if you do not have any of these issues in your life, you still need the Lord. There has to be emptiness on the inside—I know because I have been there. Everything seems to be going all right and yet something is still missing. I pray that reading this book has helped you to find that missing link.

TO MY PEERS

First, I celebrate all my fellow athletes around the world. I know the challenges you face each day. Been there and done that too! I appreciate the gift that God put in you for your profession. Yes, I believe that God gave you the ability to do what you do best. There are many other talented players in the world, but for some reason, they did not make it to where you are. As I celebrate you, I also know that things did not have to turn out the way they did for you or for me. You are blessed to represent your families, teams, cities, and even nations as you bring honor to your sport.

I encourage you to pray, attend the chapel services, love your spouse, and be examples to your children.

Let the place that God has put you on be a platform and not a pedestal. Pedestals only have room for one person. There is no room for the ones whom you love or even for God. *When you stand on a platform, it celebrates not only you, but also all that concerns you.* You can share your great moments without getting stuck on yourself. *The greatest thing about a platform is that there is room for God to get the glory.*

When God gets the glory, you can take the light of that glory home with you. When men steal God's glory, the flickering lights of fame go out, having lasted only as long as their last great moment. The person who experienced that temporary and phony glory ends up seeking that great moment for the rest of his life, never finding it and ending up unfulfilled. When God is highlighted, satisfaction is inevitable and the end is sweet.

False success is bitter! It digs a deep pit in the soul of a man because God is not his source. This is why the Bible says that it is unprofitable for a man to gain the world and lose his soul.

Too many so-called successful people end up looking for love in all the wrong places. I have looked there too—in women, drugs, and on ego trips. They only cause us to hide behind the fame of the game.

I stand by your side, as someone had to stand by my side. I speak to you from hard experience. I know the hurt and pain, and I offer to you what was offered to me. I especially speak to my brothers who struggle with male pride. Some of us were taught as little boys that we could not cry. Yet there is nothing as blessed as a man who will break down and cry before the Lord. If there is anything bottled up inside you, I pray that you will allow it to be released from you. Allow God to deal with the guilt, shame, and pain. If you are suffering from fear, let Him deal with it now.

Now find a mirror. Sit down and look at yourself in it. Are you struggling with an identity crisis? With all the great things going on around you, do you know who you are looking at in that mirror?

Let me offer this answer. You will never be able to relate to who you are until you can relate to who Christ is.

Close your eyes and allow God to fix what's missing in your life. This will not be another temporary fix received from women, money, material things, or even the rush that you get when you play the game. Bask in the presence of the Lord as He sets your heart toward the thing that will last forever.

One of my favorite Scriptures is 2 Peter 3:9: "The Lord is not slack concerning His promise, as some count slackness, but is longsuffering toward us, not willing that any should perish but that all should come to repentance." These are God's words to us that He is faithful to anything He promises.

I have experienced this truth in my life. God has been faithful to me, and I pray that my testimony will prompt you to prove His faithfulness in your life. He is not slack when it comes to His promises. This means that not only will God bless you, but also that He will bless you good!

One final comment, though: a relationship with God is based on *covenant*. God wants you to repent of your sins. *Repent* simply means "change and go the other way." God wants you to put Him first and show your loyalty to Him. So I encourage you not to seek love in the wrong places. God does reward those who diligently seek Him!

To Every Reader of This Book

In closing, I give you an invitation to find what I have found. If you do not know Jesus Christ as your Lord and Savior, I invite you to pray this simple prayer with me:

> *Father God, in the name of Jesus, I repent of my sins. I invite You into my life and give You permission to be Lord over every area of my life. Teach me Your Word and Your ways so that I can be a witness for You in the earth. Amen.*

Maybe you are a believer, but you have not walked in the promises of God. Maybe you've slid down that slope away from God. If you put yourself in either of those categories, pray this prayer with me:

> *Jesus, I renounce every error of my ways, and I submit to Your Spirit. I separate myself from any person, place, or thing that would hinder my faith walk. I commit my life to obedience in prayer and the discipline of studying Your Word.*

Now be prepared. God will make Himself known to you. I promise. More than that, *He* promises!

A PRAYER FOR YOUR DESTINY

Are you still uncertain of your destiny? God says, "Call to Me, and I will answer you, and show you great and mighty things, which you do not know" (Jer. 33:3).

I have found that to be true!

I have made it through some challenging things in my life. Before I knew how to pray, someone was praying for me. Our lives are predestined and foreordained. Most people do not understand God uses the power of our words to come in agreement with what He has laid out for us already. This is why I believe in praying prayers that bring the will of God down from heaven to Earth. I call these "destiny prayers."

You can pray the prayer below for yourself, for your family members, and for your friends. This prayer came out of some of the challenges that I have faced.

I pray that as you too speak these words, the doorways to the traps that I fell into will close. There is life and death in the power of the tongue. As you pray this prayer, speak life to the will of God, and speak death to anyone or anything that would come against it.

The Bible says the devil is defeated by the blood of the Lamb and the word of our testimony. This book does not say, "Look at David!" It gives my testimony so that young people can read about my life and know that they can have victory over anything that antagonizes their destiny. From reading this book you should have a revelation that there are enemies assigned against every destiny that God has ordained.

My testimony takes the power of those enemies away and reinforces new testimonies. The real power of a testimony is its ability to bring forth more testimonies. May you fight the good fight of faith concerning your destiny and get stirred up to tell your testimony too!

Pray this prayer aloud:

> *God, I thank You for the impartation of vision that I have received from reading the testimonies in this book. Anything that would send distraction to my mind concerning my destiny is no longer a factor in my life. I receive endurance and steadfastness to finish my course. I confess that Your kingdom has come so that Your will can be done in my life. My feet are anointed to stand and to move forward in the promises that You have for me. I will not be blinded by the false lights of the earth that will shine my way. The gates of my life are open so that the King of glory can come in and have His way. Lord, You reign in my life! The showers of blessing rule over my house, and these blessings are running me down and taking me over. I am contagiously blessed, and my generations are reaping the harvest of these blessings. I will inherit that land that You have so graciously given to me. Wherever the soles of my feet shall tread, according to my inheritance, the land belongs to me. I will not be moved by enemies in my land.*

I declare that no weapons formed against me will prosper. I am loaded daily with the blessing of the Lord, and no curse shall abide in my house. I drink the cup of the blessing, and I am fat with destiny. God, You knew my way before I was formed in my mother's womb. I thank You that as I follow Your way, You will make my way prosperous. I speak life to the years ahead of me. My latter end shall be greater than my former. I fully expect the miracles of God to be my portion.

Lord, You have caused Your face to shine upon me, and I submit to be used to make Your way known in the earth. I renounce the prosperity of material things without the prosperity of my soul. Because I have this balance in my life, the nations will call me blessed. My name has gone before me. Word of my breakthrough has gone forth in the spirit. My blessings cannot be blocked!

Lord, You have made my name great, and I will continue to glorify Your name under its covering. You favor me because my enemies do not triumph over me. This favor will take me into my destiny. Every enemy of my destiny is under my feet. Victory is mine! I will not die hard, and my life will not go unfulfilled. Every dream and vision that God has for my life will prosper. Poverty, lack, failure, and doubt have no place in the plan of God for my life. They are displaced by prosperity, abundance, success, and faith, in Jesus's name!

Lord, I thank You for every level of increase I experience in my family, business, career, and personal life. Thank You that You are bringing me into new levels of deliverance. I have godly balance in my life, and I am living in my set time of favor. Nothing from my past can plague my present life or detour my future. The latter rain of the Lord is ruling over me and all that concerns me. My dry season is over! Every challenge in my life has been fuel for success.

My hands are anointed! Everything I do will prosper. I am strategically lined up with the will of God. The beauty of the Lord is the root of my favor, and it will never run out. Uncommon blessings are upon me and mine. Extraordinary doors are swinging off the hinges on my behalf. On a daily basis I will eat boldness for breakfast, the power of God for lunch, and humility for dinner. Because of this, the testimonies of the Lord will have a domino effect in my life.

Father God, I commit to seek Your will and the things of Your kingdom before anything else in my life. My children will reap the benefits of this obedience. They will follow the path that I have laid out and rise up and call me blessed. Let the words of my mouth and the meditation of my heart be acceptable in Your sight as I submit this prayer. My destiny is in Your hands. Amen.

NOTES

CHAPTER 3
TRAVELING DOWN THE WRONG TRACK

1. Albany.edu, "Sourcebook of Criminal Justice Statistics Online," http://www.albany.edu/sourcebook/pdf/t4252006 .pdf (accessed May 22, 2008).

CHAPTER 11
A SUPERNATURAL BOWL

1. Judy Battista, "Giants Stun Patriots in Super Bowl XLII," *New York Times*, February 4, 2008, http://www.nytimes .com/2008/02/04/sports/football/04game.html?scp=4&sq= david+tyree&st=nyt (accessed May 18, 2008).

2. Jarrett Bell, "Super Bowl XLII Ups and Downs," *USA Today*, February 4, 2008, http://www.usatoday.com/sports/ football/nfl/2008-02-04-bests-worsts_N.htm (accessed May 18, 2008).

3. Ben Walker, "David Tyree's Circus Catch Saves Giants," ABCNews.com, February 4, 2008, http://abcnews.go.com/ Sports/wireStory?id=4236481 (accessed May 18, 2008).

4. Ibid., http://abcnews.go.com/Sports/WireStory?id=4236481 &page=2 (accessed May 18, 2008).

5. Mike Reiss, "'The Catch' Won't Haunt Harrison," *Boston Globe*, June 1, 2008, http://www.boston.com/sports/football/patriots/articles/2008/06/01/the_catch_wont_haunt_harrison/?page=2 (accessed June 16, 2008).

6. Super Bowl XLII, http://www.nfl.com/superbowl (accessed May 22, 2008).

7. Exclusive David Tyree Interview, AOL Video, http://video.aol.com/video-detail/exclusive-david-tyree-interview/959638489 (accessed May 18, 2008).

CHAPTER 15
PHYSICAL AND SPIRITUAL DISCIPLINE (PART 1)

1. Kimberly Daniels, *Give It Back!* (Lake Mary, FL: Charisma House, 2007), 123.

2. Ibid., 120–122.

CHAPTER 16
PHYSICAL AND SPIRITUAL DISCIPLINE (PART 2)

1. "The War on Fat: Spiritually and Physically Fit" is used by permission of Kimberly Daniels.

CHAPTER 18
FROM MY HEART TO YOU

1. Thomas P. Boncz, "Prevalence of Imprisonment in the U.S. Population, 1974–2001," U.S. Department of Justice, Bureau of Justice Statistics Special Report, August 2003, http://www.ojp.usdoj.gov/bjs/pub/pdf/piusp01.pdf (accessed May 22, 2008).

2. Fox Butterfield, "Study Finds Big Increase in Black Men as Inmates Since 1980," *New York Times*, August 28, 2002, http://query.nytimes.com/gst/fullpage.html?res=9C04E6DD 1F3CF93BA1575BC0A9649C8B63&False (accessed May 22, 2008).

3. U.S. Department of Justice, "Criminal Offenders Statistics: Characteristics of Jail Inmates, Substance Use and Treatment," Bureau of Justice Statistics, http://www.ojp.usdoj .gov/bjs/crimoff.htm#jail (accessed May 22, 2008).

4. Boncz, "Prevalence of Imprisonment in the U.S. Population, 1974–2001."

5. Ibid.